DIGITALIZATION OF BUSINESS PROCESSES

A Systems Approach

L.R. Chary
Mallika Ladi

BlueRose Publishers
NewDelhi • London

First Published in January 2022

ISBN: 978-93-5472-853-2

BLUEROSE PUBLISHERS

www.bluerosepublishers.com
info@bluerosepublishers.com
+91 8882 898 898

Cover Design:
Aveek

Typographic Design:
Rohit

Distributed by: BlueRose, Amazon, Flipkart

"Aa no bhadraah kratavo yantu vishvatah"

"Let noble thoughts come to us from every side"

-Rigveda 1-89-1-

PREFACE

The last two decades have witnessed winds of change blowing across the corporate world and bringing about dramatic transformation. First, it was the Acquisitions and Mergers (A&M) wave followed by the Total Quality Management (TQM) and the Six Sigma et al wavelets. Then arrived the tidal wave called the internet which broke all the geographical barriers and gave birth to two new concepts of doing business, namely, e-business and e-commerce. These changes have forced entrepreneurs and businessmen alike to re-orient and re-adjust their ways of doing business, which, in management parlance, are referred to as Business Process Re-engineering (BPR) and Corporate Transformation (CT). The fast changing business environment has also brought in a new set of business terminologies, some of which are alien even to a veteran businessman, And what is more! Now the COVID 19 pandemic has added yet another dimension to the way of doing business,namely, Work From Home (WFH) requiring for this purpose seamlessly integrated end-to-end digitalization of business processes.

Taking advantage of the rapid developments in the corporate world, certain over-enthusiastic professionals have gone overboard prescribing drastic and at times unwarranted changes to the existing business processes and practices even without properly understanding them. They seem to believe that high-tech solutions are the only panacea for the ailments afflicting the present day businesses. The hype about technologies and tools being the sole cure for all corporate illnesses has reached such a pitch that the real issue, namely, the technique of doing business to beat the competition,i.e., the domain knowledge, is forgotten, altogether. In the prevailing environment, businessmen are constantly on the look out for saner counsel to find practical solutions to enable them to face the severe competition created by the globalisation of the economy.

In this context it can be seen that in the past two decades several organizations,in all earnestness, have gone in for the implementation of ERP in their respective organizations, but with mixed results.Wherever the implementation has not produced the desired results, the client organization has invariably blamed the implementer of ERP for the failure to deliver the deliverables while the ERP software implementer has blamed the client organization for not being able to specify exactly what they want and thus the blame game goes on. The real reason,however, for the failure of ERP lies neither with the client nor with the implementing agency/ software company.**This failure is attributable to the lack of a standard approach or methodology to describe the business process in an unambiguous manner so that the ERP implementer and his client organisation are on the same page.It is therefore felt that an Out-of-the-Box solution is the need of the hour, hence this work. This work,*inter alia,* suggests a systems approach to the implementation of ERP so that there is no communication gap between the implementer and the client and the project is implemented successfully to everyone's satisfaction.**

It is truism to say that systems engineering, the forebear of systems approach, is a heavy subject for a lay person to comprehend. Therefore, in order to make the systems approach concepts easily accessible to non-specialists, liberal use of diagrams, illustrations and sketches including those with allegoric references to characters from the great Indian Epic Ramayana, have been made in this work to convey the message, vividly, albeit, in a lighter vein.

The purpose of this work is to:

-Clear the air of all the confusion created by the management buzzwords and jargon;

-Explain in simple language, with the help of sketches and diagrams, the modern business concepts such as ERP, SCM, CRM etc.,

-Show with an example from real life, how organisations with legacy systems can implement MIMOCODSS - an enterprise wide IT solution for management information and decision support.

- Suggest a simple systems approach for the implementation of ERP .

Further, in this work ,case studies and examples are presented that are based on Artificial Intelligence(AI)/Machine Learning(ML) and other related techniques for the prediction of the future trends of businesses,Also presented here are ERP case studies using the systems approach, in order to make the book up to date and contemporary in nature.

Mumbai

NOVEMBER 2021

AUTHORS

GLOSSARY

AI	-	Artificial Intelligence
A&M	-	Acquisitions and Mergers
BPA	-	Business Process Analysis
BPI	-	Business Process Integration
BPO	-	Business Process Outsourcing
BPR	-	Business Process Re-engineering
BPS	-	Business Process Synthesis
CEO	-	Chief Executive Officer
CFO	-	Chief Finance Officer
CIO	-	Chief Information Officer
CRM	-	Customer Relationship Management
CT	-	Corporate Transformation
DEEPAWALI	-	An Indian Festival of Lights
EDP	-	Electronic Data Processing, Every Day Problem
ERP	-	Enterprise Resource Planning Easy Route to Prosperity, Eternally Recurring Problems
GBPR	-	Government Business Process Re-engineering
GMDB SYNDROME	-	Gharki-Murgi-Dal-Baraabar syndrome (A Hindi metaphor used to describe a tendency to underestimate what is easily available even if it is intrinsically valuable.)
GSP	-	Guru Shishya Parampara
HANUMAN	-	Lord Rama's principal devotee known for his immense strength and ability to fly
HRD	-	Human Resources Development

IT	-	Information Technology
JAMBUVANT	-	A wise and well informed character in the Great Indian Epic Ramayana
LPG	-	Liberalization, Privatization and Globalization
MATCHGLO	-	<u>M</u>arket driven, <u>T</u>echnology savvy, <u>C</u>ustomer focused, <u>H</u>uman resources friendly <u>Glo</u>bal <u>O</u>rganisation
MICARD	-	Motivated, Independent, Capable, Acceptable, Respected and Disciplined
MIMO SYSTEM	-	<u>M</u>ultiple <u>I</u>nput <u>M</u>ultiple <u>O</u>utput <u>S</u>ystem
MIMOCODSS	-	Multi-Input, Multi-Output, Controllable and Observable Decision Support System
MIMOCOS	-	<u>M</u>ulti-<u>I</u>nput, <u>M</u>ulti-<u>O</u>utput, <u>C</u>ontrollable and <u>O</u>bservable <u>S</u>ystem
ML	-	Machine Learning
PDCA	-	Plan, Do, Check and Act
SCM	-	Supply Chain Management
SISO SYSTEM	-	<u>S</u>ingle <u>I</u>nput <u>S</u>ingle <u>O</u>utput <u>S</u>ystem
SWOT	-	Strengths, Weaknesses, Opportunities and Threats
TCO	-	Total Cost of Ownership
TQM	-	Total Quality Management
WFH	-	Work From Home

CONTENTS

A Confused CEO

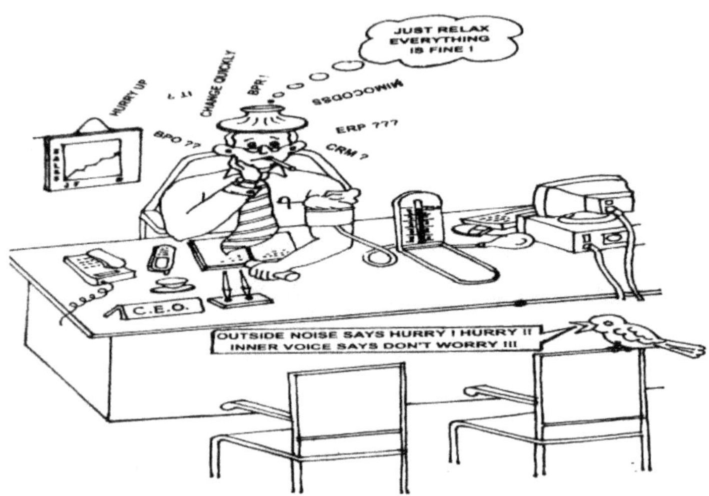

1

CHANGE - THE ONLY CONSTANT

1.1 Introduction

LPG - no! not the cooking gas, but Liberalization, Privatization and Globalization - has brought about a number of welcome changes in the industrial scenario of developing countries, the most important of which is the change in the mindset of entrepreneurs. This has engendered the new attitude that they have to be better than the best to survive in business. This very thought of survival in the face of global competition, has prompted many entrepreneurs to review their respective existing business processes and re-engineer them to face up to the challenges with confidence. It has also forced the entrepreneurs to make maximum use of Information Technology (IT) to stay ahead in their respective businesses.

A natural outcome of all these developments is the sudden growth in the number of firms which claim expertise in all the conceivable fields of business, be it in the manufacturing sector or in the service sector or, for that matter, in governance. LPG has also thrown up a new breed of professionals, armed to the teeth with jargon and buzzwords, moving about in the corporate world with a WE-KNOW-IT-ALL air, hard selling ERP, advising SCM and CRM and recommending BPR and BPO, all in one breath, even before introducing themselves properly and exchanging normal pleasantries. Such is the impact of the sweeping changes that LPG has brought about that even a seasoned businessman with a roaring business, is made to sit up and think, often with a sense of suspicion and guilt, whether his business is really doing well or whether it requires to be re-engineered.

It is a well known fact that all business processes have legacies behind them and one needs to have a profound knowledge of the business process,namely, the domain knowledge, even before entertaining the thought of business process transformation. Hence, the urgent need even for a veteran businessman to first understand what these buzzwords really mean, assess the impact such changes will have on the existing business and then take an appropriate decision. Despite all the hype and hoopla about modern business management techniques, a seasoned businessman will always rely on his experience, domain knowledge and gut feeling for making business decisions. He cannot be easily swayed with the usage of management jargon and buzzwords. However, he still needs to know what these new terms and concepts mean and what impact, if any, they can have on his business. Keeping this scenario in view, an attempt has been made here to explain some of the terms and concepts.

Any established business is bound to have tested and proven legacy systems in place. When such an organisation decides to go in for a standard ERP package for setting up an enterprise wide IT solution, it finds itself in a situation where its business processes and systems do not fit into the standard ERP package. To help such organisations find a tailor-made solution, a methodology used in control systems analysis and design is suggested here. Known as MIMOCOS, this model provides a base for business process analysis, re-design , synthesis and integration. For illustration purposes, a practical management information and decision support system called MIMOCODSS which uses the MIMOCOS design model, is presented in the 9th chapter of this book.

DAD, THIS IS MR. WILSON,. AN ERP EXPERT. HE IS HERE "TO TRANSFORM OUR COMPANY". AND DAD, BACK IN STATES ALL ARE GOING IN FOR ERP.. EVEN JONES & CO. HAVE GONE FOR IT
BUT SUNNY, WE DON'T NEED ERP, OUR BUSINESS IS FINE.
XYZ COMPANY
SALES/ PROFITS
MONTHS
...BUT SIR, YOU MUST BECOME A GLOBAL PLAYER.
MR. WILSON, OUR PRODUCTS ARE ALREADY SELLING IN ALASKA & ZIMBABWE

1.2 <u>An Entrepreneur's Dilemma</u>

It is said that old habits die-hard, but if old habits are good habits, then why should they be allowed to die? Much the same can be said about good business practices and the need to preserve them.

Just as it takes millions of years and extreme pressure equivalent to several atmospheres to turn carbon into diamond, good business practices also take considerable time to evolve. It would be unwise to cast off proven business practices, and introduce untested ones just for the sake of fashion or to keep up with the Joneses. It is no secret that today's business environment has become more demanding in terms of time and costs. Competitive pressures, financial constraints and external threats have never been greater than what it is today. That is why business also needs to be on demand. This may sound simple but being truly prepared for the transformation and maximizing its benefits, is quite a task.

Business transformation or corporate transformation (a buzzword to make it sound more awe inspiring) in simple terms, means, reviewing the existing business process and its sub-processes, redesigning or re-engineering the same, if necessary, and IT enabling the process, to meet the demands of the business environment in terms of time and costs. But, to transform or not to transform is the question. LPG, however, does not offer any option but to go in for a corporate transformation in order to remain in business. Having thus taken a bold as well as difficult decision to go in for a corporate transformation with possibly, a proviso to retain some or all of the existing tested and proven legacy business practices, certain preparatory steps are required to be taken before launching the project.

1.3 <u>Pre-Launch Preparation</u>

Prior to embarking on the Corporate Transformation Project, it is of utmost importance that a SWOT analysis of the entire organisation departmentwise/divisionwise in general and that of the IT department in particular is done. This exercise would enable the organisation to ascertain not only the strengths and weaknesses in the business process but also that of the personnel working in the various departments of the organisation. This exercise will enable regrouping, retraining and redeployment of the human resources to make the project a success.

The next important task is to identify those business processes and sub-processes which are to be retained as they are; those that are to be re-engineered and retained; and finally those that are obsolete and need to be discarded. This entire operation is a part of business process re-engineering which is discussed in later chapters of this book.

Business Process Re-engineering logically will lead us to the question - What is to be done with the legacy systems?

1.4 <u>Legacy Systems</u>

Business processes of an organisation which have evolved over a considerable period of time and, as computerisation was introduced, have been automated, are referred to as legacy systems. These could consist of business software programs for batch processing, on-line processing or stand-alone processing.

As a part of the transformation process, an inventory of the legacy software is made with the ultimate objective of integrating them to meet partially or totally, the requirements of the business environment.

1.5 <u>Mindset Change</u>

Historically, computerisation in large organisations started with automation of its accounting system. Thus the computer department or the EDP department as it was conventionally referred to, was always a part of the accounts department of the organisation. As a result, the EDP department became an island within the Accounts department with the EDP personnel marooned on this island, all the while developing application software exclusively for the accounts department. However, when an enlightened management discovered that computers could also be used to automate other business processes like personal information system etc., the scope of work of the EDP department got enlarged with other department staff coming to the EDP personnel with inputs and carrying away reams of paper as output. What is to be noted here is the fact that the EDP personnel were always approached by the personnel of other departments for automating their respective business processes and not the other way round. This feature or characteristic led to what is termed as the EDP mindset. Despite the sea change that has taken place in the computer and IT world, this mindset of the EDP staff, unfortunately, continues to exist, though, to a considerably lesser degree. For carrying out a corporate transformation, the mindset of the IT personnel has to change totally. IT department personnel should see themselves as members of a service department and reach out to help end user departments in identifying and automating the business processes.

An exercise should be undertaken to thoroughly brainwash the IT personnel, particularly those who belong to the old school and have a typical EDP mindset. The message that, in today's competitive world, the customer is king, must be permanently ingrained in their minds. They should be made to believe that the customer i.e., the end user of the software, is their very raison d'etre and must, therefore, be fully satisfied with the software. The software developers must be made to understand that their task does not end with mere designing and development of software. On the contrary, it just about begins there and gets completed only when the end user of the software becomes fully conversant with it and is able to make full use of all the features built in it in a comfortable manner.

Another change that is required to be brought about in the IT department pertains to training. Each and every developer in the IT department must be regularly sent for training to enable him to acquire the latest skill sets required for the development of software. Upon his return from training, he must be made to put the new skills to use by making him review and redesign the existing application software. Large gaps between training periods for developers become hurdles in the business transformation process, as software developers are key players in this effort.

1.6 <u>Documentation</u>

For attempting a corporate transformation and IT enablement of a large organisation, one of the important pre-requisites, is the documentation pertaining to operation/conduct of the business. This pre-requisite assumes all the more significance when the organisation in question has a large number of legacy systems. And, invariably, absence of such documentation, especially those pertaining to EDP/IT, is very common. Even in organisations where documentation is available, these will be in the form of scraps of papers on which the system specifications, patches etc. would have been just scribbled and the papers filed in a haphazard manner. One should not be surprised to find software patches written on the back of old grocery bills, bus tickets etc. About user manuals for the end user of the software, such a concept seldom exists even in an organisation in which an EDP/IT has been in existence for decades.

The prime reason for such a state of affairs is, perhaps the existence of Guru-Shishya Parampara (GSP) in the EDP/IT departments. Under the GSP the team leader or senior software professional (Guru) will pass on information (system specs., design details, flow chart, coding etc.) pertaining to a project, in bits and pieces to his junior (shishya), most of the time, orally. The Mool Mantra here seems to be "INFORMATION IS POWER, SO DON'T PART WITH IT EASILY". Under these circumstances, the mover & shaker or the change agent who wants to effect a corporate transformation has his task cut out for him. Regularly updated documentation is the bedrock of a good business process.

1.7 <u>Top Management Support And Leadership</u>

For a victory in war, the army, navy and airforce chiefs are required to work in close co-ordination. Although corporate transformation is not a war, yet it demands no less an effort from the three chiefs of the organisation, namely, the Chief Executive Officer (CEO), the Chief Finance Officer (CFO) and the Chief Information Officer (CIO), to make the project a resounding success.

The CEO is the prime mover of the project. The responsibility of making available the right men, money and material for the project, squarely rests on his shoulders. He is also required to motivate and galvanise the entire organisation into action. For the success of the project, the credit may or may not go to him but for its failure the blame will definitely get shifted onto his shoulders. Not at all an enviable position to be in but that's the price one has to be prepared to pay for being the CEO.

For executing the project in time, smooth flow of funds is a prime requirement. The CFO's greatest contribution to the success of the project would be to promptly ensure unhindered flow of funds,while ensuring that the money is spent properly.

While the roles of the CEO and the CFO are largely confined to the management of the project at the macro level, the CIO's role includes both the macro as well as the micro levels of management of the corporate transformation project. This places an enormous responsibility on the CIO for which he must be fully equipped.

When asked to suggest the right qualifications and qualities for the position of CIO, an HRD consultant put it thus - "besides having a fairly sound knowledge about the hardware, software, middleware and networking together with adequate basic engineering skills, your CIO must also be a MICARD professional". When queried further, the HRD consultant went on to explain thus: "Effecting even a small change in a business process is a big challenge because of its far reaching consequences. Attempting a corporate transformation is a bigger challenge, which calls for a well co-ordinated team effort. In this effort the role of the CIO, who is the captain of the team, is very crucial, for this individual can either make or mar the project. MICARD stands for <u>M</u>otivated, <u>I</u>ndependent, <u>C</u>apable, Acceptable, <u>R</u>espected and <u>D</u>isciplined. A professional possessing these qualities alone can motivate

GURU-SHISHYA PARAMPARA IN EDP DEPARTMENT

and bring the best out of each and every member of the project implementation team".

Any change is a challenge and not many like it. The mere mention of a change in the work environment is greeted by the staff with a howl of protest. And in addition, if a suggestion is made, particularly to the in-house IT professionals, that an external agency is likely to be commissioned to guide them in the software development activity, the protest turns into a demotivation factor for the staff members, sometimes leading to loss of self confidence in themselves. Under these circumstances, the CIO will find it almost impossible to function.

In such a situation the CIO will be required to assume the role of Jambuvant and remind his IT professionals about their strengths and capabilities to accept the challenges offered by the change. (In the famous Indian Epic Ramayana, it is narrated that when Hanuman was instructed by Lord Rama to go to Lanka to ascertain the whereabouts of Sita, he did not know what to do or how to proceed and was therefore very depressed. It was Jambuvant who reminded Hanuman about his immense strength and ability to fly that finally got him going).

In short, the Chief Information Officer has to play multiple roles of a leader, friend, philosopher and guide and, if situation demands, the role of Jambuvant too, in order to get his team going.. He is the king-pin on whom the success of the corporate transformation project hinges

2

BUSINESS PROCESS RE-ENGINEERING

2.1 Introduction

Having dwelt at length on the task of preparing the major change agents for carrying out business transformation, the task now is to attempt a business process re-engineering (BPR). But before attempting a BPR, the existing process needs to be studied and analyzed in depth with a view to ascertaining its strengths and weakness vis-a-vis those of the competitors. In addition, the analysis should also reveal gaps between the practices of the business under study and the best practices in the field. Such an analysis would then give the right inputs to synthesize a properly re-engineered process. Thus, for effective BPR, the organisation must first draw up a list of existing functionalities of the business process along with a wish list of functionalities it desires to have to make the business process better than the best benchmarked business process in the field. An analysis of the gap between these two lists will serve as the base for arriving at the specifications to effect the BPR.

2.2. Domain Knowledge - An Essential Pre-Requisite For BPR

Man has been doing business since the dawn of civilization. Businesses have been conducted on the basis of certain rules, procedures and practices, all of which undergo change from time to time and also from place to place, thus suggesting that business processes are evolutionary in nature resembling a Markov process. In other words, all businesses have legacies behind them and one needs to have a thorough and profound knowledge of the process even before entertaining the thought of effecting a change in the process. Hence, the need on the part of an entrepreneur to first understand thoroughly the technique of doing business before venturing to re-engineer it.

The art of managing business is acquired by an entrepreneur either from his own experiences or by being an apprentice to some one who already possesses this art. It is thus, by and large, a practical, time consuming learning process and, therefore, cannot be acquired overnight. There is no FAST FORWARD button to help accelerate the learning process for you, nor is there a Business school any where in the world which can help you in this effort. Remember, experience alone is the best teacher. On the subject of learning business management, this is what Henry Mintzberg, Cleghorn Professor of Management Studies at McGill University, has to say: "Giving young people, who have never managed, the impression that we are turning them into managers is very dysfunctional. Even taking people who are managers and doing what we do in B-schools, which is concentrate on the business function, does not teach them management. People learn business management by focusing on their own experience and learn from their own experience".

If a business process is to be re-engineered, then the person or agency intending to do so must:

1. Have a thorough knowledge (also called domain knowledge) of the process in question.

2. Be aware of the drawbacks, if any, in the existing process, and

3. Know the procedure to remove the drawbacks so that the re-engineered business process yields a guaranteed higher return than before, at minimal cost.

Employing a common procedure to re-engineer a given business process on the basis of certain superficial observations could lead to catastrophic results. For instance, although courier service, airline service and shipping service are all forms of transportation business, it would be simplistic to assume that all three are the same and use identical techniques to conduct their businesses. Further, it would be naive to believe that the methods of re-engineering the business processes too could be identical in the three cases. Hence the most important pre-requisite for re-engineering a business process is the domain knowledge. Having thus answered the question as to what is the pre-requisite for effecting a BPR, two other questions pop up, namely, whether at all it is required to re-engineer the existing process and, if required, then when is it required?

A business is considered to be doing extremely well when the productivity is higher than the productivity of all other competitors; when all customers are fully satisfied; and, above all, when the bottom line is at its zenith. Under these circumstances, one can confidently say that no re-engineering of the business process is required nor is there a need for corporate transformation. In other words, when an enterprise has become a MATCHGLO i.e., Market driven Technology savvy Customer focused Human resources friendly Global Organisation, it can be safely concluded that no further transformation is required, at least, for the time being. But when an organisation does not have any of these attributes, it means that the time is ripe for change and the organisation should seriously commence the process of corporate transformation by taking the first step, namely, Business Process Reengineering(BPR).

BPR, in simple terms, means spring cleaning of the business process or processes of an organization. In BPR all the old and inefficient processes, procedures and practices are done away with and in their place, new and efficient ones are introduced. The prime purpose of undertaking such an exercise is to provide total customer satisfaction and thereby increase the profits of the organization. While attempting a BPR, it must be accepted that the way you do business may need to change and the way the members of your organisation do their jobs may also need to change. Both these changes are bound to be painful at times and will therefore, call for tremendous amount of patience, tolerance and persuasive efforts from the top management. Any attempt by the top management to force changes down the throats of its employees especially with the advice of consultants, will prove counterproductive, if not a total disaster, benefiting only the consultant in the process. It must be understood that BPR is a continuous as well as a long drawn process and therefore can not be left to the consultant alone to do it. This is principally because the consultant can not be expected to possess a thorough knowledge, also referred to as domain knowledge, as well as experience of the business process. Experience has shown that consultants do not have the time or patience to fully understand a given business process in order to be able to find defects in it before reengineering it. Hence major contribution to BPR should come from within the organization for it is only the employees of the organization, who know the business process well in all its aspects and can contribute to make the process more efficient and effective.

2.3   Business Process Analysis , Synthesis & Integration

2.3.1. BP Analysis (BPA):

Business processes can be analyzed in a variety of ways depending on what the analyst desires to examine. However, from the point of view of BPR, an approach that is used for the analysis and synthesis of automatic control systems in the engineering field, could be of advantage, as elaborated in the following paragraphs.

Just as it is done in the case of engineering system analysis, a large and complex business process with multiple inputs and outputs is broken down into its constituent sub-processes which in turn are again broken down into smaller sub-processes or sub-sub-processes as shown in Figure 2.1.1 and Figure 2.1.2 which represents in the form of block diagrams for the large business process and the constituent su b-processes.   The sub-processes can be further broken down or split into tasks and the tasks into sub-tasks. Thus a sub-task represents the basic building block of a businesss process.

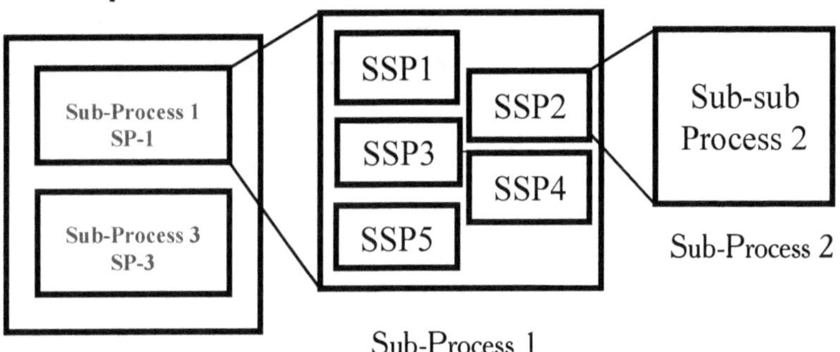

Large Business Process

Figure 2.1.1

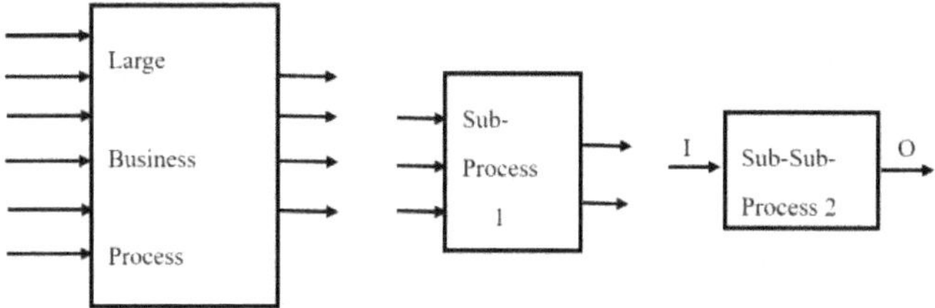

Figure 2.1.2

Each block represents a process or a sub-process with its inputs and outputs clearly identified. The contents of each block represents the tasks and the sub-tasks which transforms the input into output and is called the transfer function or the business rule. This input-output relationship through the transfer function/business rule fully describes the process, sub-process, task or sub-task enclosed within the block diagram as shown in Figure 2.1.2.

For example, consider the sub-sub-process-2 show in Figure 2.1.2. Let the input be denoted by I, the output by O and the transfer function or the business rule of the process or task be identified as K. This implies that the output O is obtained when the input I is acted upon by the transfer function K, which in other words means $O/I = K$ or $O = KI$ i.e., the output is K times the input, K being the business rule. Stated alternatively, the input is magnified or enhanced K times by the process to produce the output. For example, if we assign a numerical value 10 to K, then we can say that the output of the sub-sub-process-2 is equal to ten times the input. Although the transfer function K shown in this example is a constant, it could, in other cases, be a business rule such as a differential operator or an integral operator or even a differential equation describing the business process.

This method of analysis, using the block diagram approach, which is extensively used in the analysis of engineering processes, can be used to analyse socio-economic processes as well, including business processes. This methodology is discussed in detail later in chapter 7.

From the foregoing discussions, it can be seen that any business process can be broken up into its constituent sub-processes and the causal relationship between their respective inputs and outputs can be determined. At this stage, should it be established that a certain sub-process needs to be modified or eliminated to improve the performance of the business, then the same can be done effectively.

2.3.2 <u>BP Synthesis(BPS)</u>

Having thus re-designed the sub-process, or processes to meet certain objectives, the various sub-processes can be re-assembled to form the main business process. This procedure is termed as business process synthesis and it is in effect just the reverse of business process analysis.

2.3.3 <u>BP Integration(BPI)</u>

Business process integration follows business process synthesis. In business process integration all the sub-process blocks are arranged in logical sequence and interconnected so as to form an intregrated business process.

The entire procedure of business process analysis, synthesis and integration is called business process re-engineering (BPR).This can be expressed in the form of a simple equation, thus;

BPR = BPA + BPS + BPI　　　　　　　　　　**(2.1)**

2.4 <u>Automation Of The Business Process</u>

We have so far gone through the various steps leading to BPR and have also got a fair idea about business process re-engineering which is dealt with in greater detail, later. But re-engineering the business process does not necessarily mean automating it. At the end of BPR one can encounter the following situations:

1. A scenario where all the re-engineered business processes are manual.

2. A scenario where the re-engineered processes are partly manual and partly automated.

At this juncture the management is required to take the decision whether or not to fully automate the entire business process which, in management parlance, is referred to as Business Process Automation(BPAuto) or Digitalization of Business Process. The environment of Liberalisation, Privatisation, Globalisation (LPG), however, leaves very little to choose from, if the management's goal is to make the enterprise a MATCHGLO. Hence the Hobson's choice of going in for total automation of the entire business process. Therefore, for total Corporate Transformation it becomes necessary to provide a Seamlessly Integrated End-to-End Information Technology System(SIEEITS). The equation 2.1 above now becomes:

BPR = BPA + BPS + BPI + BP Auto   **(2.2)**

The route so far has perhaps been smooth, but it has led us to the crossroads. The dilemma faced is whether it would be wiser to go in for a ready made standard Enterprise Resource Planning (ERP) package to automate and integrate the entire business process or to evolve an enterprise wide IT solution using the in-house resources which includes man power and legacy systems. Here, it is worth emphasising that the prime purpose of automating a business process is to provide the right information to the right person at the right time for decision making and not forgetting the ultimate objective of improving the bottom line. To make the right choice one needs to know the merits and demerits of both the options.

2.5 Transformation of Government Business Processes

After LPG (Liberalization, Privatization and Globalization) a large number of companies in the private sector have changed their ways of doing business in order to be competitive in the global market place. This has forced companies in the public sector also to re-engineer their business processes in order to remain in business. But there seems to be no perceptible change in the government business processes as anticipated, despite the great emphasis laid by the government on e-governance. If all round economic progress is to be achieved briskly, then government should also re-engineer its business processes at an accelerated pace. Further, the coming into force of the Right to Information Act has not only made it incumbent upon the government to make its business processes transparent but has also forced it to make information available to the public when demanded. This is possible only if government business processes are re-designed and automated, where necessary. The National Knowledge Commission too, in a set of ten recommendations, has firstly sought government process re-engineering before computerization. An accelerated transformation of the business of governance is, therefore, the need of the hour.

2.5.1 <u>Need For An Attitudinal Change</u>

The prime requirement for bringing about changes in the government business processes is the change in the mind set of both the elected representatives of the people and the government servants. The old ideas and beliefs of the Raj era that the government is the supreme ruler and the people are its subjects, is passé. Instead, in the fast-changing global environment, the government should perceive itself as a public service provider and the citizens as its valued customers. Just as business rules are modified in BPR by companies for maximization of customer satisfaction, the law makers should change all the antiquated laws and enact new laws in their place to enable GBPR (Govt. Business Process Re-engineering) for the welfare of the people.

2.5.2 <u>A Systems Approach Based Methodology For GBPR</u>

As already stated, BPR (Business Process Re-engineering) in simple terms means reviewing the existing business processes with a view to deleting old and useless processes and practices and bringing in new ones with the ultimate objective of maximizing customer satisfaction. BPR comprises of Business Process Analysis (BPA), Business Process Synthesis (BPS), Business Process Integration (BPI) and Business Process Automation (BPAut).

In the Systems/Process approach, a process is defined as a series of sequentially arranged tasks. Each task has a well-defined set of inputs and outputs as well as a set of business rules. Thus, a task can be viewed as the basic building block of a business process/sub process, just like an atom which is the basic building block of a molecule, and the molecule which in turn is the basic building block of matter.

2.5.3 <u>Government Business Process Re-Engineering (GBPR)</u>

In the business of governance, the functioning of a ministry can be thought of as a large business process, with the departments under it as smaller business processes and wings and sections as sub-processes and tasks respectively. Each section performs a task and this can be considered as the basic building block of the GBP. To perform a task a set of inputs is essential and on completion of the task a set of outputs is generated.

2.5.4 <u>GBP Analysis</u>

In this analysis a review of a task is done with a view to ascertaining its relevance to today's concept of good governance which, in other words, means how this task will benefit the public who are the customers. Such an analysis will lead to three possible outcomes:

1. The task under review is totally irrelevant and hence must be done away with.

2. The task is partly relevant and, therefore, must be modified suitably to make it fully relevant and thereafter be retained in the re-engineered process.

3. The task is totally relevant and hence must be retained in the re-engineered business process, as it exists.

On similar lines each task is analyzed and the results of this analysis are used in the next step of the GBPR, namely, GBP Synthesis.

2.5.5 <u>GBP Synthesis</u>

The process of synthesis is basically the reverse of the process of analysis. While analyzing a business process, it is broken down into sub-processes and tasks, in the process of synthesis, the various tasks are reassembled to form sub-processes and the sub-processes are rearranged in proper sequence to form the GBProcess so as to enable it to function optimally. This process is similar to rearranging the building blocks of Lego to form a meaningful picture.

2.5.6 <u>GBP Integration</u>

The next step is GBP integration. In this, the various sub-processes and tasks are logically inter-connected to function as a seamlessly integrated business process to deliver outputs while optimizing certain specific business objective functions (attain a given set of performance indices like minimum time, minimum cost, highest quality etc.,).

2.5.7 <u>GBP Automation</u>

This is the final step in the GBPR. It means IT enablement or digitalization of the entire business process, that is, computerization of the business process using for this purpose a suitable platform and an appropriate data base.

Merely computerizing the existing processes (manual paper work) without re-engineering them will be like speeding up inefficient tasks. The mantra for successful transformation of GBP is total revamping of the existing processes with full involvement of all the people who will be using it, right from the conceptualization stage to the final implementation stage.

Any attempt to make changes to the systems and processes without making parallel changes to the mindset of the concerned people, is bound to fail before long as witnessed in the case of a number of projects of similar nature. People will develop positive attitude towards change only when they are fully involved in the transformation project right from the beginning.

It is a well-known fact that, under the e-governance programme, a number of projects have been initiated in various government departments and undertakings. But the general perception is that at no place a seamlessly integrated total IT solution has been implemented covering the entire gamut of business pertaining to a government department or undertaking.

Government departments are not alone in this predicament. Some private companies as well as PSUs that have attempted to get quick fix ERP solutions implemented without re-engineering their business processes, are also facing problems.

One could attribute the following reasons for this unsatisfactory state of affairs:

1. Computerization of the existing paper work without proper re-engineering of the business process.

2. Failure on the part of the organization to specify in precise terms its requirements to the IT experts. This is mainly due to the absence of a standard methodology for this purpose.

3. Non- involvement of the entire organization in the transformation effort right from the conceptualization stage to the final implementation stage.

4. Reluctance on the part of experts to delineate a step-by-step procedure that will be employed for transforming the business process.

2.5.8 <u>Appreciation Course</u>

Keeping in view the points mentioned above which appear to be the principal reasons for the limited success of government business process transformation projects, a short course of a day's duration is recommended. The objective of the course is to arm the participants with basic information about business process transformation, its costs and benefits, the methodology used for GBPR and above all the importance of total involvement of every member of the organization from START to FINISH. The topics to be covered in the recommended familiarization programme are:

1. Change, its inevitability and change management

2 Business Process Re-engineering – A Systems Approach (Systems Approach will enable the organization to bridge the communication gap between the process owner/user and the IT experts/developers)

On completion of the course the participants will be in a position to convey, in precise terms, the exact requirements of the business process to the IT experts for automating the process. This will also help the participants to actively participate in the project and guide it in the right direction.

3

ENTERPRISE RESOURCE PLANNING

3.1 <u>Introduction</u>

The nineties threw up quite a few buzzwords and jargon, acronyms and abbreviations which the corporate world gladly lapped up, sometimes even without understanding their meaning or implication. One such acronym was ERP which cast a magic spell over the entire corporate world in the late nineties and in the early years of the present millennium. Since then several tomes have been written on this subject. It is not the intention of the authors to overburden the reader with another exposition on ERP. However, both for the sake of completeness and for the benefit of the uninitiated, a few observations about ERP are made in the following paragraphs.

ERP meant different things to different people: Enterprise Resource Planning to some, Easy Route to Prosperity to the seller of the ERP software package, and a source of Eternally Recurring Problems to an organisation where the ERP package had been poorly implemented.

Putting things in perspective, Enterprise Resource Planning does not fully live upto its acronym. One is unable to understand why the founding fathers named it thus, as, one would realise later, this package has little to do with planning and what resources it is referring to is unclear. However, the word Enterprise in ERP seems to capture the entire spirit, purpose and ambition of this package. The prime purpose of an ERP is to integrate functionally and operationally, all the divisions, departments and sections of an enterprise into a single seamlessly welded automated system that can serve the right information or data, to the right people at the right time for decision making purposes. It may appear to be a daunting task for a single system to serve, for instance, the diverse needs of the people in the finance, HR, commercial and technical services departments, simultaneously. But this is precisely what an ERP is expected to do.

MEANING OF ERP

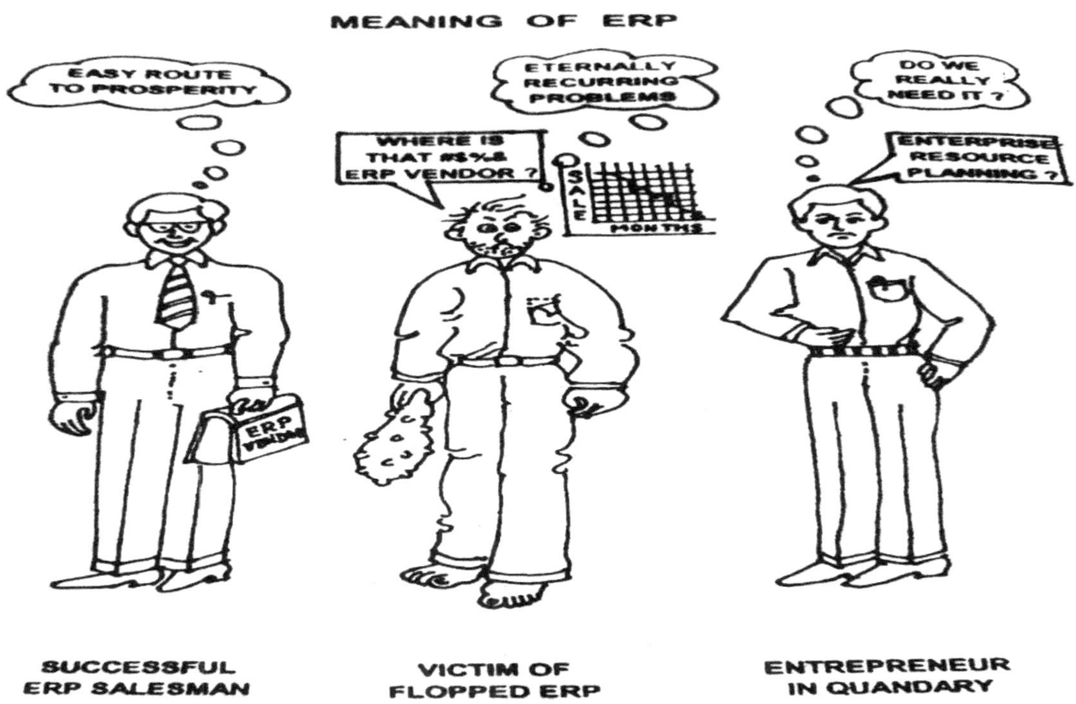

In a typically large organisation having a number of legacy systems, each department has its own computer system optimized for the particular way that the department does its work. A properly configured and implemented ERP, in this case, combines such disparate systems into a single integrated system that runs on a common database so that various departments can easily share information/data and communicate with each other. An integrated solution of this kind can have a tremendous impact on the payback or bottom line of the company.

For example, consider a ERP-less manufacturing unit handling an order. Typically, when a customer places an order, the order form with all its details gets keyed and re-keyed into various departments' computers along the way. The movement of the order form, while the order is being processed in this manner, can cause delays and loss of orders. The keying and re-keying of order information into different computers becomes a potential source of errors in the order processing operation. Meanwhile, if the customer wants to know the status of his order at a given point of time, no one in the company is in a position to give him the right information without making him run from pillar to post. This leads to customer dissatisfaction which ultimately affects the business adversely.

ERP, on the other hand, replaces all the stand-alone systems with an integrated one which runs a single unified program on a common data base. This unified program is made up of several software modules which mirror the entire business process that each stand-alone system independently ran before. In this changed environment, the various departments like finance, manufacturing, warehouse and shipping not only get their respective information about an order promptly from the system, but are also able to see the status of the order at any point of time. This enables the company to give up-to- date information about the status of an order, instantly, thereby preventing customer frustration. Further, assuming that the entire process including the human interface, works with clock work precision, the order processing operation moves swiftly through the organisation, and the customers get their orders faster with fewer errors than before. On similar lines, with the prompt arrival of error free inputs on-line, timely closure of annual accounts also becomes possible.

As can be seen from the foregoing, a perfectly implemented ERP enables an organisation to seamlessly integrate financial information, customer order information, standardize and accelerate the manufacturing

CUSTOMER SERVICE DEPARTMENT

ERPLESS COMPANY

COMPANY WITH ERP

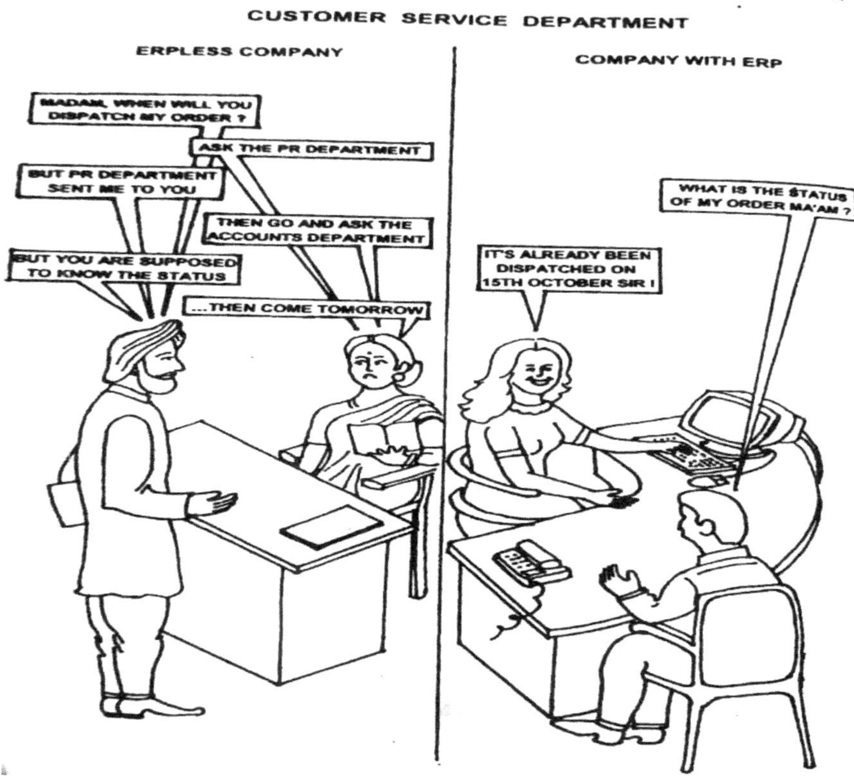

processes, optimally regulate inventory levels and standardize HR information. But is a perfect ERP implementation possible, especially, when an organisation has legacy systems?

3.2 <u>Time Required For ERP Implementation</u>

The next series of questions that automatically spring up are: How long will it take to implement an ERP? Will the old system and the new ERP system run in parallel for sometime? Is a bumpless transfer from the old system to the newly implemented ERP possible?

To answer the question about the duration of implementation, it must be said that this depends on several factors such as acceptability of this idea by the entire organisation, willingness on the part of the people to change their ways of working and readiness of the people to get trained before taking up the new ways of working. In their eagerness to sell the product, ERP vendors generally tend to give a very short average implementation time of three to six months. There is definitely a catch in this statement for, in such a short period, it may be possible to implement just one or two modules like the financials or HR but not the entire ERP. The real transformational ERP project takes a much longer duration of about three to four years for completion.

As regards parallel runs with the existing system, it is most essential to follow this procedure to ensure no disruption to the business process. No business process can afford to fully switch off the old process and then switch on the new, as such a method can lead to tremendous loss to the organisation. So, for a bumpless transfer from the old to the new, the safest way is to have parallel runs till the new system has fully stabilised.

3.3 <u>Cost Of ERP Implementation</u>

ERP implementation means providing a total IT solution which includes software, hardware, network infrastructure, professional services and training of staff. The cost for providing all the above services is generally referred to as total cost of ownership (TCO) of the ERP.

A survey of about fifty companies consisting of small, medium and large size enterprises, reveals that the average TCO is USD 15 million with the highest cost being USD 300 million and the lowest cost being USD 300,000. Whatever the size of the company, the TCO of an ERP is quite exorbitant and therefore, it calls for considerable deliberation on the part of the management and total commitment from each and every member of the organisation, before deciding to go in for an ERP.

It must also be borne in mind that the TCO figures are bound to escalate two years after the ERP implementation when the real cost of upgrading, optimizing and maintaining the system for your business show up to your utter surprise.

3.4 <u>The Hidden Costs Of ERP</u>

The most common experience of every organisation which has gone in for an ERP solution in a big way, is the problem of unestimated and unbudgeted costs. These costs, which are at times inestimable or unforeseeable or both, often running into thousands of dollars, are made up of a number of components like customization costs, integration and testing costs, data migration costs, training costs and other sundry costs all adding up to a whopping figure which can make the blood pressure of the CEO, CFO and CIO shoot up. Neither the ERP vendor nor the consultant can make things any better for you as both are blissfully ignorant of the hidden costs of ERP. Let us examine each of these hidden cost elements, which explode unexpectedly like land mines, along the ERP implementation path.

3.4.1. <u>Customisation cost:</u>

Customisation means tailoring the ERP modules in such a way that your entire business process snugly fits into these modules – a task easier said than done. This involves not only a deep understanding of the business process and its nuances by the implementer of the ERP, which is too much to expect from a mere mortal, but also extensive changes to the ERP modules themselves. And these are to be achieved without messing up with the ERP software which are all so tightly coupled that they cannot tolerate any further fiddling. This entire operation could be time consuming and therefore very expensive.

3.4.2. <u>Integration and Testing costs:</u>

Close on the heels of customization costs follow the costs involved in integrating and testing of the various ERP modules alongwith other corporate software links including legacy software. It is very common for a manufacturing unit to go in for a range of software packages like Supply Chain Management (SCM) software, Customer Relationship

Management (CRM) software and a host of other packages required for computing Goods and Service Tax(GST) and other taxes. All these software packages are required to be integrated with the ERP modules appropriately. If such packages come, preferably from the same ERP vendor, in a form that they can be straight away plugged into the ERP system, then the problem of integration gets considerably reduced. But if the SCM, CRM and other utility packages are to be sourced from disparate vendors, then the integration of these with the ERP system could prove to be a nightmare. Whatever the option chosen, integration of add-on software packages with the ERP system is unavoidable and has, therefore, to be done with abundant caution to prevent a major mess up.

It is customary for the IT personnel to test the integrated system module by module using dummy data for this purpose. This method is efficacious only in the case of a simple system. Men wizened by experience, however, recommend an end-to-end run with real data, before going on stream, mainly to avoid any unpleasant surprises. To sum up, integration and testing are both time consuming and painful and hence cost quite a packet.

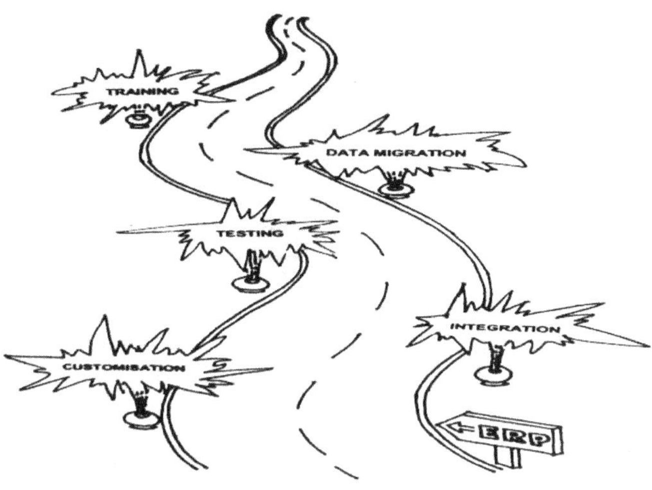

3.4.3 <u>Data Migration:</u>

When an organisation migrates from an old legacy system to a brand new ERP system, one of the most important and yet, the least remembered activity is data migration. For instance, when a manufacturing unit chooses to go in for a brand new ERP system, enormous amounts of data and information, such as customer and supplier records, product design specification data, HR information etc. need to be moved from the old system to the new. This movement of information and data costs money. While small companies use this as an excuse to junk old data, large organizations like insurance companies and banks which have several pending claims and recovery cases, cannot afford to do so. Migration of data in such cases becomes a very expensive but necessary exercise, not normally reckoned while budgeting for an ERP project. There are organizations, particularly in the service sector, which routinely perform extensive analysis of data for planning and forecasting purposes. In such organizations the data from their ERP systems often require to be combined with data from other external systems for the purposes of analysis. While preparing a budget for the ERP system, these organizations should include the cost of data warehousing also. Updating or refreshing all the ERP data on a daily basis in a large corporate data warehouse is a difficult task and the ERP systems are not well equipped to indicate which information has changed from day to day, thus making selective warehouse updates very tough. Perhaps custom programming could solve this issue but at an exorbitant cost.

3.4.4. <u>Training costs:</u>

Training of staff is the most important, the most sensitive, the most expensive and yet the most underestimated item in an ERP budget. The training expenses are very high because each and every member of the staff is required to learn a new set of business processes and new way of working. It is not merely learning to use a new piece of software but learning a whole new approach to conducting business as it were and hence the high cost. In this training effort, outside training agencies and institutions are of little or no help, as these outfits can, at best, teach how to use a new software but not educate your staff about the particular way you have to do business in the new ERP environment.

Training is also a very sensitive issue as the people to be trained will belong to wide ranging age groups and educational backgrounds and having diverse skill sets. Complicating this issue will be the attitude of the learner. For instance, an experienced staff member may adopt a DON'T TRY TO TEACH VETERANS LIKE US HOW TO DO BUSINESS attitude. Or for that matter, a well educated new entrant youngster may quiz the very need for a HARVARD or a STANFORD returned like him to learn the elementary principles of doing business. All the while both these categories of staff may not even be aware of what an ERP is and how it can help the business. Keeping in view the various problems and pitfalls associated with training of personnel to make them ERP savvy, it is advisable for the organization to develop its own training programmes. While preparing the course material for training, the following points need to be kept in view:

1. The curriculum should give a total picture of the entire business process to the participants.

2. The curriculum developed should be able to identify and explain the different sub-business processes that will be affected by the new ERP system.

3. It should give a broader understanding of how others in the organization will be doing their jobs vis-à-vis the earlier practices.

4. The participants must be able to appreciate the fact that all the departments like HR, finance, marketing, accounts etc. will be using the same software and will be keying in data/information into the system that will affect the others.

As already mentioned the prime responsibility of training should rest with the IT and business operations people of the company as such a type of training is similar to on-the-job training for which domain knowledge is essential. However, as some enterprises have done, staff from business schools could be roped in for assistance in designing the course and the delivery system, so as to make it both efficient and effective.

The foregoing discussion makes it amply clear that training of staff could be expensive and is invariably given little or no attention while budgeting for an ERP system. When questioned about the budgetary allocation required for ERP training, an exasperated CEO of a company, said rather wryly,- "Take whatever amount you have budgeted for ERP related training and triple or even quadruple it, still you will find yourself woefully short of funds. But remember, however much you spend on training, it is still worth it".

Training, as outlined above is, beyond doubt, a very important part of an ERP implementation. But equally, if not more important, is the documentation in the form of user manuals. It would be childish to expect your staff to finish a week's training on a Saturday and start working as an ERP expert from the following Monday. Training is a continuous process and after the initial classroom training, every staff member should be provided with a well written user manual to help him discharge his daily duties efficiently. The user manual should be written in such a simple language that even the most uninitiated is able to do his work after reading the manual. But there is a cost element attached to the preparation of such a user manual, so ensure that this cost is included in the cost of training.

ERP TRAINING

4

POST IMPLEMENTATION BLUES

4.1. <u>Great Expectations and Terrible Let Downs</u>

Your business process has been reasonably well mapped on to an ERP package which has been successfully implemented, your staff has been trained and are raring to go, and it is going to be roses and roses all the way for you. Don't get misled into believing that this is going to happen easily and that everything is going to be hunky dory from now on. On the contrary, you are likely to be in for a rude shock, when it is reported that the business has, in fact, plummeted. A survey of Fortune 500 companies, that had gone in for ERP, indicates that more than 25% of the companies suffered a dip in performance when their ERP system went on stream. The main reason for this state of affairs is the loss of familiarity experienced by the staff members. In the new ERP environment everything looks different and works differently from the way it did before. When the staff members cannot do their jobs in the way they are used to and have not yet mastered the new ways of working, panic sets in, and the business goes into a tailspin. Don't press the panic button yet! All this is happening because Murphy's Law – "THINGS TAKE LONGER THAN YOU THINK" – is not only in operation, but is also working overtime to frustrate you. It is commonly observed that a company which is used to traditional forms of software project management, expects to gain instantly from any new software installation. This, unfortunately, does not happen with the ERP system. A majority of the ERP systems do not yield the desired results for a considerable period of time. The company will be able to reap the benefits of ERP only after it has been finely tuned and the staff members are able to comfortably use the system just as they did with the old system. Till then patience is advised.

4.2. <u>Team Disintegration Threat</u>

Normally when an organization decides to implement an ERP system, it selects the best of talents available within the company to form the core implementation team. This team is associated with the project right from scratch and continues till the implementation is completed, successfully. At the end of the project each and every member of the team naturally becomes an expert in his own right and is normally sought after by other organisations and ERP consultancy firms who try to snap up these veterans with tempting offers to which most fall prey. It, therefore, becomes a difficult task for the company to retain these worthies, especially when the HR policy of the company prevents it from giving them a better counter offer. It is painful for the company to see these experts leave but even more painful it is for the company to hire other experts to replace them at much higher costs. It would be wiser for the management to formulate a more flexible HR policy so as to be able to retain the in-house ERP veterans. For this to happen the management must first stop suffering from the GMDB (Gharki-Murgi-Dal-Baraabar) syndrome and accept the fact that their own staff members are as competent (if not, more) as the outsiders who claim to be ERP experts.

4.3. <u>Follow-up Folly</u>

Most organizations tend to treat their ERP project like any other software project. In any software project, once the project team has completed the installation and commissioning of the software, the company normally breaks up the team and the members of the team are sent back to their respective parent departments to resume their old jobs. But in the case of ERP, if the same practice is followed, then it could prove to be a disaster as many companies have experienced it , to their dismay.

The team that has implemented an ERP system is too valuable to be wasted away thus. As the team has worked very closely with the ERP system right from its conceptualisation to final implementation, the members tend to know more about the entire business process. For instance, they will know more about marketing and sales than the regular marketing and sales staff, and more about finance and accounts than the accountants. Hence, the company simply cannot afford to break up the ERP team and send the team members back to their respective old jobs. The team will have to be retained to carry out certain follow-up tasks like scripting reports to draw information out of the ERP system, conducting analysis to ensure that the company is getting its money back from the ERP installation etc. Very few IT departments plan their post-ERP implementation activities properly, with the result that what is started with a bang tends to end with a whimper and in the process sends confused signals about the success of the project.

4.4. <u>Long Wait for the Elusive Fruits of Labour</u>

It is but natural for a company to expect return on its investment. "The quicker the return the better" is the watch word. But no such thing applies to ERP. As already explained, Murphy's law works overtime in the case of ERP system. Till such time the entire system is finely tuned and the end users are able to use the system, comfortably, the company has no other choice than to wait patiently for the expected returns.

4.5 <u>Failure of ERP</u>

The ERP system is supposed to be the mirror image (without the lateral inversion, of course!) of the business process of an organization. Its success depends on how thoroughly the business process has been understood by the implementer and how accurately the business process has been mapped on to the ERP software package. A poorly implemented ERP due to lack of understanding of the business process (this is the most common cause for many a ERP failures) is no better than the legacy system it is supposed to replace. On the contrary, in many cases, ERP system is worse than the legacy system, because, in the case of a legacy system, the old codes and practices have evolved over a period of time and have been written specifically for a company and its tasks and can still deliver results which may not be optimal, though. A mad rush into ERP implementation without understanding the nuances of the business process will lead to more FLOPS than HITS. Further, it must be understood that every business is different and is bound to have unique work methods and culture of its own, which an ERP vendor cannot easily reflect in the system when customizing a standard ERP software. Another factor which contributes to the failure of ERP is the unrealistic assumption that most of the companies make regarding changing the work habits of the staff. The management feels that it is far easier to change people's work habits than to customize the ERP software and sets about the task only to realize soon that this is next to impossible. If the staff is resistant to change, then the ERP project is bound to fail. To sum up, the main reasons for the failure of ERP projects, are:

1. Lack of domain knowledge of the business process on the part of the
    implementer/vendor of the ERP system

2. Lack of total acceptance to change on the part of the staff of the
    organization.

3. Misplaced "ONE SIZE FITS ALL", belief of the ERP vendors
    and consultants.

4. Attempts to modify the core ERP software to fit an organization's
    work methods, and in the process making the software unstable and
    difficult to maintain.

5

METHODS OF ERP IMPLEMENTATION

5.1 Introduction

Once a decision has been taken to implement a standard ERP package, the question then arises as to how to go about it. From a study carried out, there appears to be three basic approaches for the implementation of an ERP project.

5.2 The Big Bang Approach

As the name suggests, you start this project with a bang. This is the most ambitious yet the most difficult of the three approaches, as it is a high handed approach, directly mandated by the Chief Executive of the organization. If it fails, it is bound to invite criticism for being both a dictatorial as well as a cavalier approach. In this method of implementation the company junks all its legacy systems and installs a single standard ERP system across the organization at one go. Most of the initial ERP implementations across the globe followed this method and quite a few came a cropper. One of the main reasons (besides lack of domain knowledge) being, that this method calls for the entire organization to mobilize and change overnight in unison, which is asking for too much. Expecting everyone in the company to cooperate and accept a new, untested software system requires tremendous effort, mainly because there is no one in the organization who can vouch for its efficacy due to lack of adequate experience. No one in the company is sure whether the new system will work or not. In an environment where many departments have specially tailored computerized systems that have been fine tuned to match the way the staff works, the new ERP system will demand compromises, which will lead to clashes. This is because, in almost all the cases, the new system offers neither the range of functionalities nor the comfort of familiarity that a custom built, finely honed legacy system offers. One of the main casualties of such an implementation is the speed of operations, which is severely affected as the new system tries to serve the entire organization instead of a single

THE BIG BANG APPROACH

department. Only the bravest of the brave will opt for the big bang approach.

5.3 <u>The Conservative Approach</u>

True to its name, this approach is bereft of any flamboyance and instead is full of caution. This method of ERP implementation is generally resorted to, by large and diverse organizations which do not have many common features between various business units and which still believe in retaining some proven legacy systems. In such an organization, independent ERP systems are installed in each business unit while linking common business processes like finance and accounting, across the organization. Usually in this type of implementation, a business sub-process, which will not ordinarily disrupt the entire business process when something goes wrong with it, is selected as a pilot unit and an ERP for this specific unit is implemented. Upon successful implementation of the pilot ERP unit, replication of this scheme is carried out selectively on other sub- processes. Although this approach takes a long time for completion, it does not cause any major hiccups to the entire business process. Companies that go in for this approach for implementing ERP, believe in the maxim, IT IS BETTER TO BE SAFE THAN SORRY.

5.4. <u>Snug Fit Approach</u>

It is said that the most perfectly implemented ERP project is the one in which the business process fits into a standard ERP software like a glove. In other words, the implementer has been able to accurately map the business process on to the ERP package, without either re-engineering the business process or modifying the software. As one expert chose to put it thus – "the business process should fit into the ERP software so well as to feel AS SNUG AS A BUG IN THE RUG" . Such instances are few and far between, and are found generally in smaller organizations. The aim here is to get the ERP up and running as quickly as possible which naturally means minimum, if not, no changes at all, either to the process or to the ERP product – a CANNED, END-TO-END solution of sorts. Such a solution is generally found to be a bit better than the legacy system it replaces , as it does not force the employees to change their old methods of working. But the payback, in this case is small. It is also said that the management of the company which opts for this approach, does so with the sole objective of being recognised.

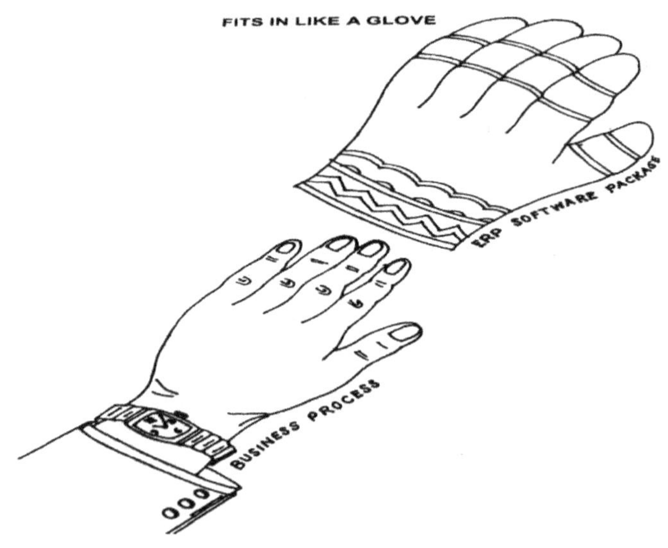

6

ERP'S COMPANIONS

6.1 <u>Introduction</u>

ERP is not the only one to take the corporate world by storm. Two junior companions of ERP that created ripples alongwith ERP software packages are SCM and CRM. Some insights into these two country cousins of ERP, as some experts choose to call them, are given here.

6.2 <u>Supply Chain Management</u>

Supply Chain Management (SCM) is the art of improving the way of procuring the inputs to produce a product, manufacturing that product and delivering the finished product to the customers. The five basic components are: Planning, Sourcing, Manufacturing, Delivery and Feedback. Alternatively, a supply chain can be thought of as a network of facilities and distribution options that performs the functions of procurement of materials, transforming these into products and delivering them to the customers in the most efficient manner. Supply chains exist both in the service and manufacturing organisations, with the complexity of the chain varying greatly from industry to industry and from firm to firm.

Though every manufacturer of goods or provider of services has been having some form of supply chain for his business from the very beginning of commerce and has been managing it ever since, all that the SCM software does is to leverage the attributes of IT to optimize the supply chain, thus making the process more efficient. However, SCM has its own pitfalls. For example, a supply chain planning software is much better at managing growth than it is at monitoring a decline and correcting it. Also, to get your supply chain partners to agree to collaborate with you, you have to be willing to compromise and help them to achieve their own goals. If the supply chain system is difficult on the outside, it is not any easier on the inside either, as people working for an organisation are normally comfortable with a certain way of working which reflects the character of the organisation that is difficult to change overnight. Hence, the low success rate of SCM software.

6.3 <u>Customer Relationship Management</u>

Successful businesses depend on creating long-lasting relationships with customers and this is precisely what Customer Relationship Management (CRM) is all about. Research shows that it often costs five times more to win a new customer than it does to keep an old one. Therefore, adding value to the existing customers can be a very profitable investment. For this, it is important to identify your best customers. In most distribution companies, the thumb rule is that just 20% of the customers account for 80% of the profits. CRM software helps to analyse a company's customer base by producing accurate ranking reports, thus enabling the company to focus on maximizing satisfaction among the key customers. For less important or less profitable customers, the system helps by suggesting different buying patterns, order volumes and price structures to make the partnership a more profitable one.

While the CRM software can be useful to the extent of business information about a customer which gets fed into the system, it cannot, however, take care of the customer's moods, likes and dislikes and the peer pressures, all of which have a bearing on the customer's behaviour pattern which ultimately affects the decision making process. Hence, the need to have a thorough knowledge of the business as well as the individual customers who can affect the business.

It is also worthy of mention here that no software package can be bought off the shelf and used straight away. The package has to be customized to suit a particular client's business needs. A near-perfect fit is possible if the package is implemented along with the commencement of the new business. This brings us back to the question - what then is the solution for old businesses which have legacy systems in use? The answer perhaps lies in the MIMOCODS system, the design of which is based on modern control system design principles which is discussed in chapter 9.

SCM IN ACTION

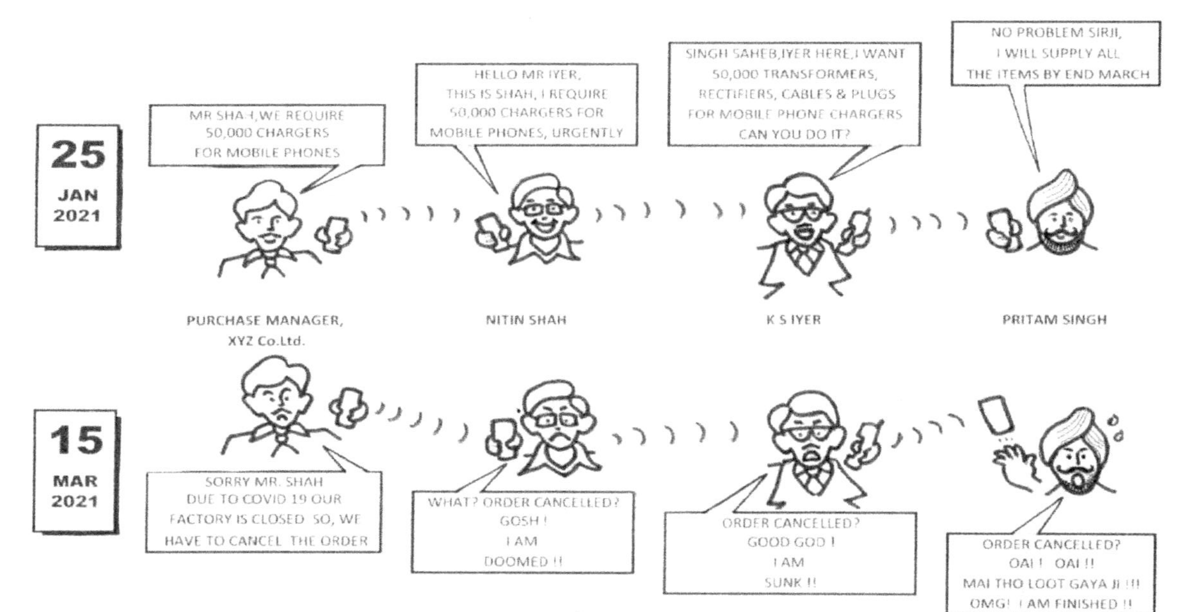

CUSTOMER RELATIONSHIP MANAGEMENT

6.4 <u>ERP and E-Commerce</u>

Except for the alphabet E, there is very little in common between ERP and e-commerce. ERP is a complex system meant to be exclusively used by trained staff within an organization and is not intended for use by the public at large. When an ERP system is implemented in, say, a manufacturing organisation, it is assumed that the only people handling information pertaining to an order will be the staff who have been trained for the purpose and are comfortable with the software as well as the jargon associated with ERP. However, with the heralding of e-commerce for which the ERP systems were not originally designed, customers and suppliers of the organization have started demanding access to the same information that the staff of the organization gets from the ERP system such as order status, inventory levels etc. They also expect this information to be made available to them through the organization's website in as simple a manner as possible, devoid of any jargon associated with the ERP software.

If an ERP system is required to cater to the needs of e-commerce, then your IT department must arrange for two new channels of access to your ERP system – one for your valued customers (also known as business-to-consumer link) and the other for your suppliers and partners (business-to-business link). The types of information sought by these two categories of people differ greatly. While the consumers will ask for the order status and billing information, your suppliers and partners will expect to know just about everything else. These developments have become a cause for concern for companies with e-commerce ambitions. The IT departments of such companies are required to put in a lot of effort to make their ERP systems available on the Web. For those companies that were fortunate to buy the ERP systems from the vendors who had capabilities to develop suitable e-commerce software, it became as simple as buying the e-commerce software modules from the same vendors and plugging them into the respective ERP systems. But the unlucky ones had to really sweat it out to make their ERP systems, e-commerce compatible. All said and done, integration of ERP system with e-commerce is quite a task and will require careful planning to get it going in the right direction.

Another tricky aspect of this marriage between ERP and e-commerce is the one concerning maintenance and availability. While, on the one hand, internet website which is directly linked with ERP, must be available 24 x

7, on the other hand, ERP applications which are generally large and complex, require periodic maintenance and will have to be delinked from the web for this purpose. This conflict is usually resolved by building flexibility into the ERP and e-commerce links, so that new e-commerce applications are kept running on the web while the ERP is shut down for upgrades and maintenance work.

In order to get over the difficulty of getting ERP and e-commerce applications to work together harmoniously and also to enable ERP to provide information demanded by its companions SCM and CRM, the IT industry has come up with a software generally referred to as middleware. Middleware functions as software translator and converts the information from ERP into a suitable format that is easily understood by e-commerce, SCM and CRM. Middleware is invisible to computer users and has proved to be very useful in solving the integration problems faced by the IT industry.

7

METHODOLOGY FOR BPR

7.1 <u>A Control Engineering/Control Process Approach</u>

We have so far seen what corporate transformation is all about and how it involves business process re-engineering and IT enablement. We have also been introduced to ERP, SCM, CRM and e-commerce concepts and how these in the form of standard packaged solutions also contribute to corporate transformation. However, what appears to be missing in this exposition, is a mention about the procedure one needs to follow to re-engineer a business process.

Is there a standard procedure for analyzing a business process to identify its strengths and weaknesses prior to re-engineering? Is there a standard way to synthesize the business process? How does one integrate and automate the re-engineered business process? These are some of the questions that arise when an entrepreneur contemplates a corporate transformation. In this context it would, perhaps, be wise to turn to the field of automatic control system engineering for some clues.

Feedback, one of the most fundamental processes existing in nature, is present in almost all dynamic systems, including those within men, among men and between men and machines. As a result, the theory of feedback control systems, also sometimes referred to as automatic control systems, has been developed as an engineering discipline for analyzing, synthesing and designing practical control systems and automated devices. Recognition that this theory is directly applicable to formulating and solving problems in many other fields such as economics, sociology, business and commerce, is becoming widespread. It is no surprise when a professor of economics discusses feedback controls in an economic process. Nor is it any more a matter of wonder, when a social scientist talks of closed loop interaction between different societies and groups.

As the dynamics of any business process involves the process of feedback among people, all the tools of analysis and synthesis that are used to study automatic control systems, become applicable to business systems as well. Before venturing further with the analysis and synthesis of business systems, it is necessary to understand certain basic concepts of control systems.

7.2 <u>Basic Concepts Of Control System Or Process</u>

Control systems (or processes) abound in man's environment. These systems could be engineering systems, biological control systems, economic control systems or business systems. But before amplifying on this, two terms, which help in identifying a control system, namely, the INPUT and the OUTPUT, need to be defined.

1. INPUT is defined as a stimulus or excitation applied to a control system from an external source, in order to produce a specified response from the system.

2. OUTPUT is the actual response obtained from the system. This output may or may not be equal to the specified response implied by the input. If the output and input are given, it is possible to identify or define the control system and its components or sub-systems. Control systems can have more that one input or output. Often all inputs and outputs are well defined by the system description.

There are three basic types of control systems:

1. Man-made control systems – Example: Thermo-statically controlled room heating system.

2. Nature made control systems which includes biological control systems – Example: Perspiration control system in human beings to maintain body temperature.

3. Control systems whose components (or sub-systems) are both natural and man-made. Example: Man driving a car. This has components which are both man-made (ie., car) and natural or biological (i.e., man).

7.3 <u>Classification Of Control Systems</u>

Control systems are classified into two general categories, namely, open loop and closed loop control systems. The distinction is determined by the control action or the input, which is that entity responsible for activating the system to produce the desired output. The two categories of control systems are defined thus:

1.   Open-loop system: An open-loop system is one in which the control action or input to the system is independent of the output. Example: An automatic bread toaster.

2.   Closed-loop system or Feedback system: A closed loop system is one in which the control action or input to the system is dependent on the output of the system in someway. Example: an autopilot mechanism and the ship or the aero plane it steers is a closed-loop or feedback control system.

Closed-loop or feedback control systems are further classified into negative feedback and positive feedback control systems:

1.   In a negative feedback control system, the control action is made up of the reference input from which a part of the output is subtracted.

2.   In a positive feedback control system, the control action is made up of the reference input to which part of the output is added.

7.4 <u>Characteristic Effects Of Feedback</u>

The presence of feedback in a system has certain characteristic effect on the performance of the system as enumerated below:

1. Increased accuracy, i.e. the ability of the sytem to faithfully reproduce the input.

2. Reduced sensitivity of the ratio of output to input to variations in system characteristics.

3. Reduced effects of non-linearities and distortions.

4. Tendency towards instability.

7.5 <u>Analysis And Synthesis Of Control Systems</u>

Two types of problems are normally encountered in control systems engineering design and they are analysis and synthesis of a control system configuration.

Analysis is defined as the investigation of the properties of an existing system with a view to improve its performance whereas synthesis or design is the choice and arrangement of the control system components (or sub-systems) in order to make the system perform a specific task to yield optimal results.

7.6 <u>Representation Of A Control Systems Problem</u>

In order to solve a system problem, the description or specifications of the system configuration and its components (or sub-systems) must be cast into a form which makes it amenable to analysis, design and evaluation.

In the study of control systems, three basic methods of representation (or modelling) of physical systems and their components (or sub-systems) are extensively employed.

1. Mathematical modelling of the system

2. Block diagram representation

3. Signal flow graph representation

Mathematical models, in the form of system equations, are employed where detailed relationships are required. Every control system can be characterized, theoretically, by a set of mathematical equations. The solution of these equations represents the behaviour of the system. At times, when it is difficult, if not impossible, to find a solution, certain simplifying assumptions are made in the mathematical description. For a large number of control systems these simplifications enable the systems to be described by ordinary linear differential equations, solutions for which can be found in any standard textbook of mathematics. In this exposition, however, mathematical representation will be kept to the minimum.

Block diagrams and signal flow graphs are shorthand representations of the physical systems and their components (or sub-systems) or the set of mathematical equations which characterize them.

In this book, the block diagram methodology of system modelling or representation will be extensively used as this not only adequately describes the control system or process, but is also easily comprehensible.

Modern control systems engineering lays major emphasis on the development of mathematical models to represent physical systems. Mathematical and physical principles are also used to understand the characteristics of feedback control systems as they relate to the transmission or processing of the abstract quantity information. Control systems engineering, therefore, embraces within its scope, not only the entire spectrum of engineering sciences, but also the biological as well as social sciences which includes the science of business management.

8

BLOCK DIAGRAM REPRESENTATION OF SYSTEMS

8.1 <u>Basics</u>

A block diagram is a shorthand, pictorial representation of the cause and effect relationship (or causal relationship) between the input and output of a system. It provides a convenient and useful method for characterizing the functional relationships existing among the various components (or sub-systems) of a control system. Sub-systems or system components are sometimes called elements of the system.

The simplest form of the block diagram is the single block with one input and one output as shown in Figure 8.1. As a rule the input must enter the process block from the left hand side and the output must emerge from the right hand side of the process block as shown in the diagram.

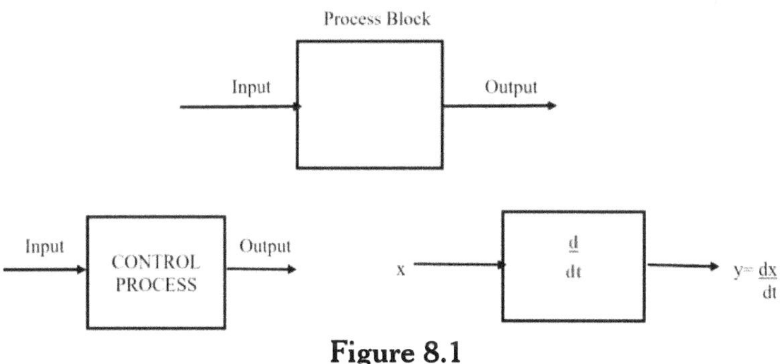

Figure 8.1

Figure 8.1 represents block diagrammatically a <u>S</u>ingle <u>I</u>nput, <u>S</u>ingle <u>O</u>utput system also referred to as SISO system.

The arithmetical operations of addition and subtraction have a special representation. The block in this case becomes a small circle, called a summing point, with plus or minus sign appropriately associated with the arrows entering the circle as shown in Figure 8.2. The output is the algebraic sum of the inputs.

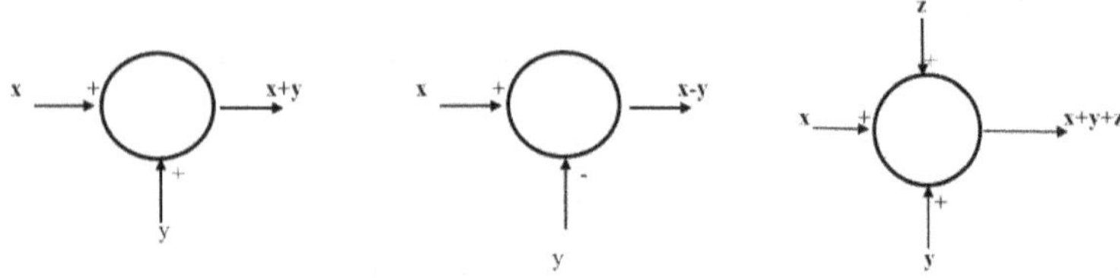

Figure 8.2

For using the same signal as an input to more than one block or summing point, a takeoff point is used as shown in Figure 8.3. This permits the signal to proceed unaltered along several different paths to several destinations.

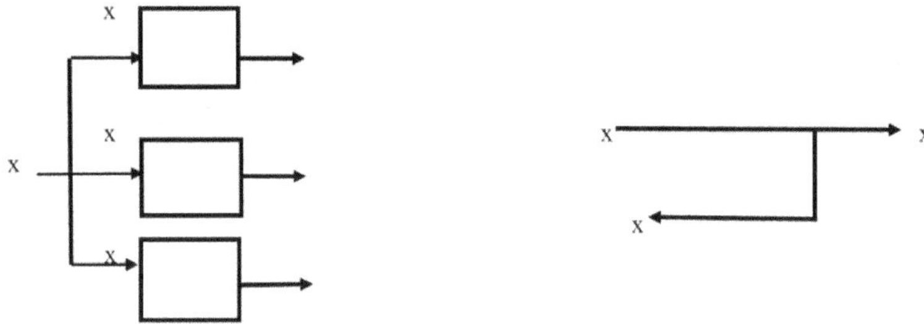

Figure 8.3

Block diagram can also be used for representing a Multiple Input, Multiple Output system as shown in Figure 8.4. Such a system is also known as MIMO system.

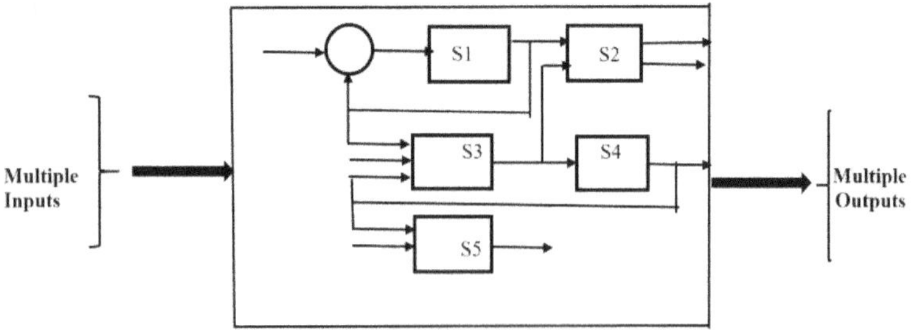

Figure 8.4

Figure 8.4 shows a MIMO system which is made up of a number of components or sub-systems which have been labeled as S1, S2, S3, S4 and S5. As can be seen each of these sub-systems in turn have either single input and single output or multiple inputs and multiple outputs.

8.2 <u>MIMOCOS</u>

We have seen how control systems are defined in terms of the number of inputs and outputs such as SISO system and MIMO system. Another dimension has been added by modern control theory, to the definition of a control system in respect of its controllability and observability. Modern control theory defines a control system not only on the basis of the number of inputs and outputs such as SISO or MIMO system, but also on the basis of the controllability and observability of its inputs and outputs, respectively. Thus, we have controllable and observable systems, uncontrollable and observable systems etc. All man-made systems or processes, be it engineering systems or socio-economic systems, fortunately fall under the category of controllable and observable systems

As any business process normally involves multiple inputs which are controllable and multiple outputs which are observable, it can be classified as a <u>M</u>ulti <u>I</u>nput – <u>M</u>ulti <u>O</u>utput, <u>C</u>ontrollable and <u>O</u>bservable <u>S</u>ystem, MIMOCOS for short.

We have now been introduced to certain basic concepts of control systems or processes. It has also been demonstrated how a system or a process can be represented in the form of a block diagram. Some examples of control processes would now be in order, to illustrate these concepts. While there are examples galore of engineering control systems, the number of examples of socio-economic systems represented block diagrammatically are few, perhaps, because this methodology of representation is not very common among economists, social scientists and businessmen. Some typical examples are presented here.

8.2.1. <u>The Price Regulatory System</u>

According to the Law of Supply and Demand in classical economics, the market demand for an item decreases as its price increases and the market supply of an item increases as its price increases. The Law of Supply and Demand states that a stable market price is achieved, if and only if, the supply is equal to the demand.

The manner in which the price is regulated by the supply and the demand can be described using certain control systems concepts. Let us choose the following four basic elements (or sub-systems) for the control system, namely, the Supplier, the Demander, the Pricer, and the Market where the item is bought and sold. These elements generally represent very complicated processes. The input to our economic system is price stability. A more convenient way to describe this input is zero price fluctuation. The output of this economic system is the actual market price.

This system is a single input single output system and therefore, can be represented block diagrammatically as shown in Figure 8.5

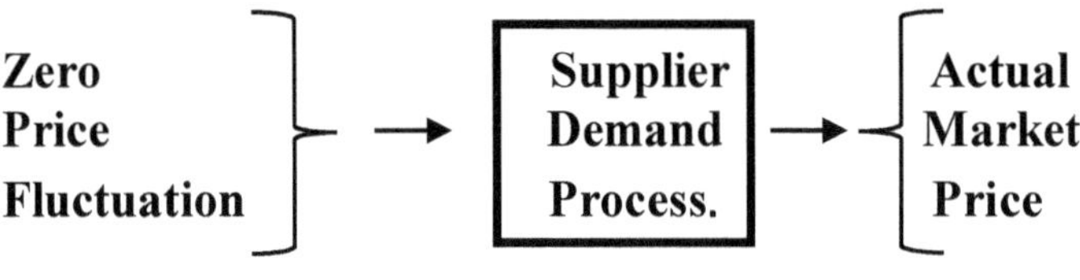

Figure 8.5

The single process block shown in Figure 8.5 can be broken down into its constituent sub-process blocks as shown in Figure 8.6 which is the block diagram of the economic process of Supply and Demand.

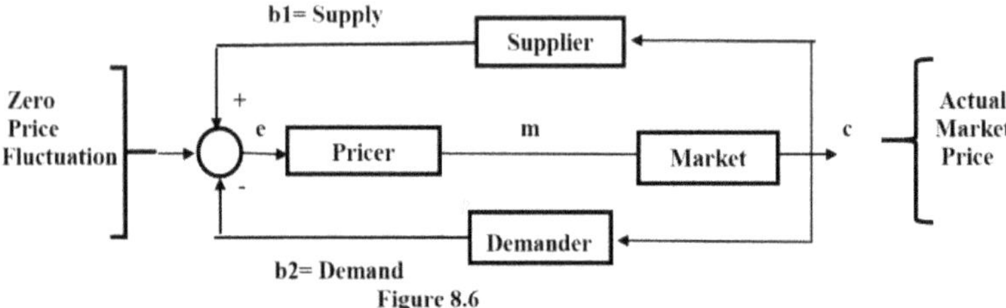

Figure 8.6

The system operates as follows: The Pricer receives a command (zero market price fluctuation) for maintaining price stability. It estimates a price for the Market transaction with the help of information from its records of past transactions. The price causes the Supplier to produce and supply a certain number of items and the Demander to demand a certain number of items. The difference between the supply and the demand is the control action for this system. If the control action is non-zero, that is, if the supply is not equal to the demand, the Pricer initiates a change in the market price in a direction which makes supply eventually equal to the demand. Hence, both the Supplier and the Demander may be considered as the feedback signals, since they determine the control action.

8.2.2. <u>The Knowledge Assessment System</u>

A knowledge assessment system is another example of a feedback control system meant not only for assessing the knowledge of the students but also for obtaining the views of the students about the role played by the teacher in imparting knowledge to them. This system can be represented by a single block as shown in Figure 8.7.

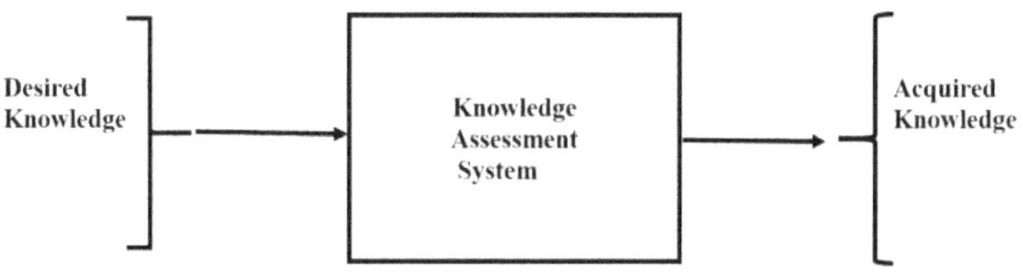

Figure 8.7

The single process block diagram shown in Figure 8.7 can be resolved into its constituent sub-systems or components as shown in Figure 8.8.

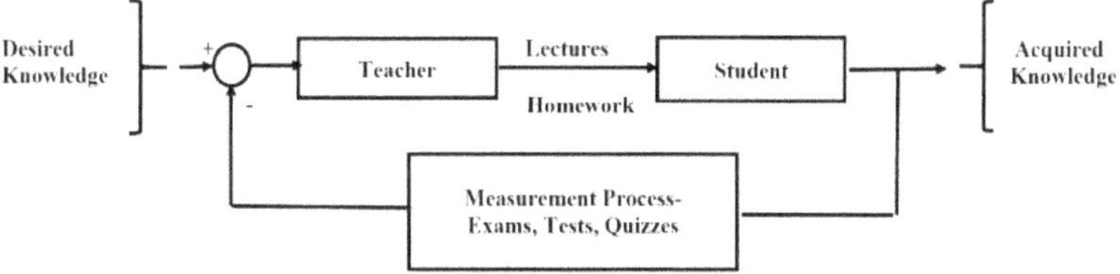

Figure 8.8

As can seen from the block diagram Figure 8.8 the teacher imparts knowledge to the student through the medium of lectures, tutorials, laboratory experiments, home- work etc. At the end of the semester, the knowledge acquired by the student is measured through the process of examinations, tests, quizzes etc. This measured information is fedback and compared with the desired knowledge information and the difference between the desired knowledge and the acquired knowledge is used by the teacher to fine tune the knowledge delivery process so as to reduce the difference between the desired knowledge level and the acquired knowledge level of the student.

8.2.3. <u>The Monetary System</u>

Milton Friedman's empirical claims about the damped cyclical response of the rate of change of national income to the rate of charge of money supply can be mathematically represented by a second order differential equation of the form.

$$\Gamma^2 \frac{d^2 x}{dt^2} + \Gamma \frac{dx}{dt} + x = m \qquad (8.1)$$

where $x = \dfrac{1}{PY} \dfrac{d}{dt}(PY)$, PY being the national income

$m = \dfrac{1}{M} \dfrac{dM}{dt}$, M being the total money supply

The above relationship between the money supply and the national income in the time domain can be represented block diagrammatically as shown in Figure 8.9.

$$\text{Money Supply } m \rightarrow \boxed{\; r^2 \frac{d^2 x}{dt^2} + r \frac{dx}{dt} + x \;} \rightarrow \text{National Income } x$$

Figure 8.9

Nachane and Chary have shown how this relationship between the money supply and national income can be block diagrammatically represented as a unity feedback control process in the frequence domain, as shown in Figure 8.10.

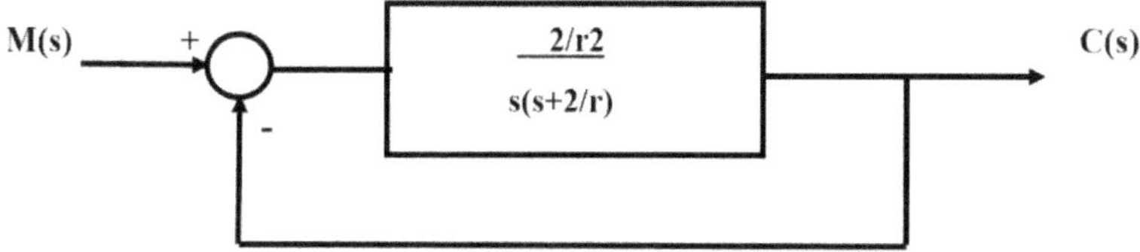

Thus it has been demonstrated that in the systems approach how a Monetary System in which the input is the money supply and the output is the national income can be effectively represented by block diagram.

THE PROCESS APPROACH

9.1 <u>Introduction</u>

The examples so far have illustrated SISO systems. We will now see what a MIMO system looks like in the form of a block diagram. But before taking up an example of MIMO system we shall briefly deviate to introduce the concept of Process Approach which is essentially the control systems engineering approach but couched in a language which has less engineering jargon in it and is, therefore, more suitable for non-engineering applications like business and commerce. In the Process Approach, a process is defined as a series of sequentially arranged activities or tasks to achieve an objective. The basic elements of a process are inputs, task and outputs as shown in Figure 9.1. The thick arrows indicate multiple inputs and outputs as per the block diagram convention.

Figure 9.1

It can be seen that Figure 9.1 is similar to Figure 8.1, the only difference being, that in the case of Figure 9.1, there are multiple inputs and outputs. Therefore, all the rules and logic applicable in the control systems approach for analysis and design are equally applicable in the case of process approach. Figure 9.2.1 and Figure 9.2.2   show hierarchical arrangements of a large business process for the purpose of analysis and synthesis. It can be seen that Figures 9.2.1 and 9.2.2 are in effect. Figure 2.1.1 and Figure 2.1.2 re-arranged hierarchically.

With reference to Figure 9.2.1, each level is a sub-process of its immediate higher level in the hierarchy i.e., each division (macro level) is a sub-process of the company, each department (mini level) is a sub-process of the division, each section (micro level)is a sub-process of the department and so on. Each sub-process has its own set of inputs and outputs which uniquely defines the sub-process. It may be noted that all business processes need not necessarily have a hierarchical structure as shown in Figure 9.2.1, but each and every process and sub-process will definitely have its inputs and outputs as shown in Figure 9.2.2.

After taking note of the striking similarities between the control systems engineering approach and the process approach and recognising the fact that they are one and the same for all practical purposes, we return to a few more examples which illustrate these approaches. We shall use the terminologies used in the process approach in these examples. Further, both the examples to be presented here will be illustrations of MIMOCOS i.e. Multi Input, Multi Output, Controllable and Observable System.

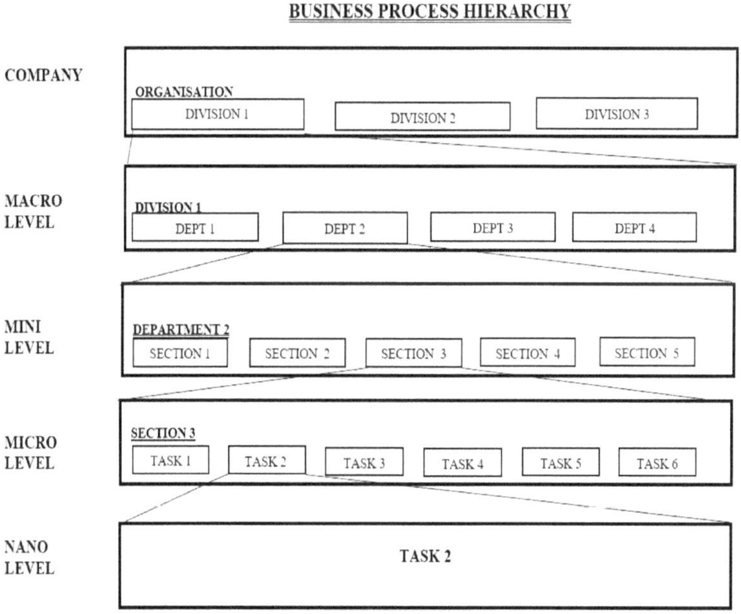

Figure 9.2.1

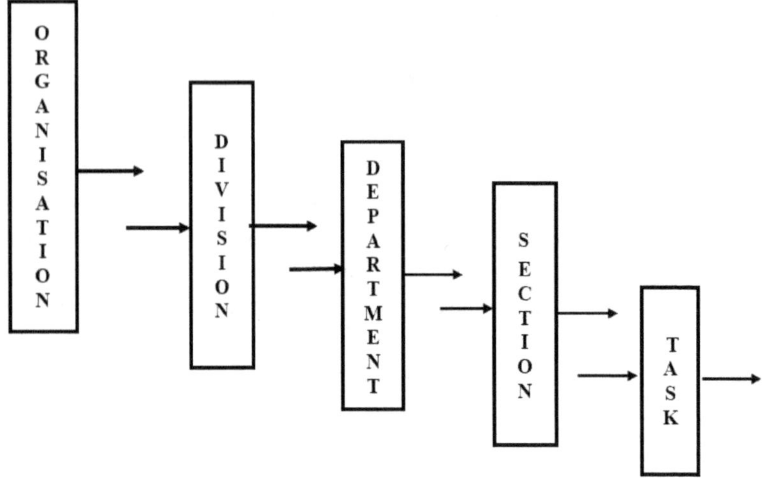

Figure 9.2.2

9.2 <u>Cargo Transportation Process By Sea</u>

The sea borne cargo transportation process is constituted by several sub-processes such as the vessel chartering sub-process, technical operation sub-process, cargo loading sub-process, voyage sub-process, cargo discharging sub-process, and the cargo delivery sub-process. A block diagram of the cargo transportation process by sea is shown in Figure 9.3.

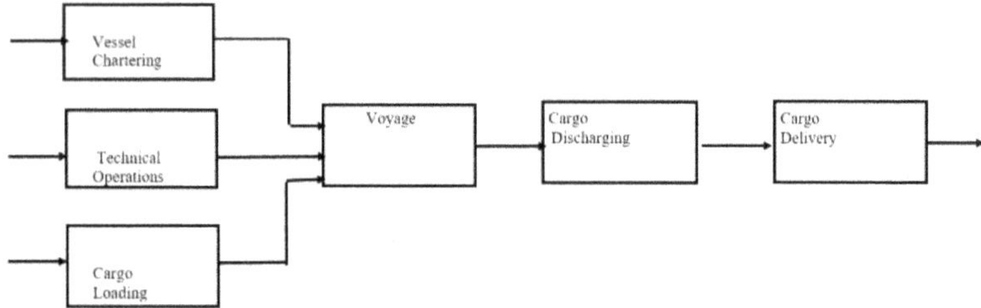

Figure 9.3

The vessel chartering sub-process involves a number of tasks which, among other things, includes drawing up the commercial parameters required for chartering, inviting offers, drawing up the charter party agreement and selecting the appropriate vessel for the voyage. The technical operations include ship's maintenance, and safety monitoring. The cargo loading sub-process includes moving the cargo to the appropriate berth, stevedoring, loading on board as per the cargo plan, and documentation. The voyage sub-process includes all the activities and tasks directly pertaining to safe navigation and carriage of cargo across the seas. The cargo discharging sub-process involves berthing the vessel, stevedoring and offloading the cargo. The cargo delivery sub-process includes all the tasks pertaining to moving the cargo outside the port for delivery and documentation related to delivering the cargo to the consignee. Needless to state that each sub-process or task is defined by a set of inputs and outputs and each one, therefore can be described by a block diagram.

9.3. <u>The Deming Quality Control Process</u>

This process which is also referred to as the Deming (PDCA) cycle, is another example of a feedback control process in the form of a Multi Input, Multi Output, Controllable and Observable System (MIMOCOS) model. A block diagrammatic representation of this process is shown in Figure 9.4.

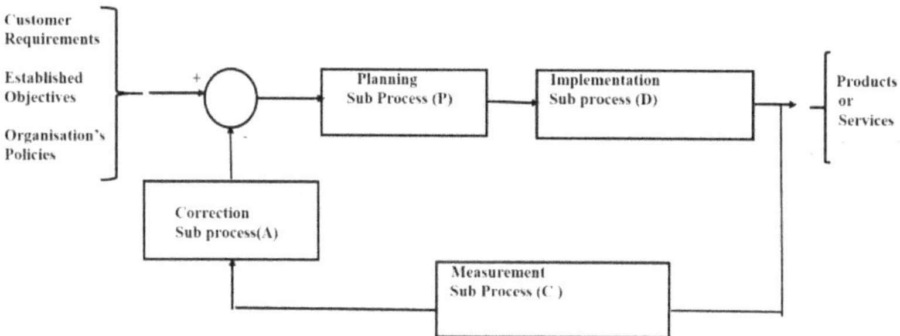

Figure 9.4

The Deming (PDCA) quality cycle consists of four sub-processes, namely, Planning (P), Implementation (D), Checking (C) and Correction (A) sub-processes.

The Planning sub-process, implies establishment of objectives and procedures necessary to deliver results in accordance with the customer's requirements, within the framework of the policies of the organization and the established objectives.

The implementation sub-process represents the 'DO' part of the PDCA cycle.

The measurement sub-process represents the 'Check' part of the PDCA cycle. Here the product or service is measured against the standard policies and objectives of the organization as well as the requirements of the customer and the results are fedback to the correction sub-process. The correction sub-process, based on the feedback from the measurement sub-process, takes action to continuously improve the process performance namely, the product or service. This sub-process is the 'Act' part of the PDCA cycle.

9.4. <u>MIMOCODSS</u>

The success of a business venture largely depends on the ability of the businessman to take the right decision at the right time, assuming that the businessman has a complete and profound knowledge of the business process and the business environment. In this information age a businessman will require a system which will enable him to quickly sift through a maze of information to arrive at the right decision. A standard ERP no doubt fits the bill provided the business process in question can be mapped perfectly on to the ERP package. But what is the alternative if the business process, especially one with a large number of legacy systems, cannot be mapped accurately on to a standard ERP package? The answer to this seems to lie in MIMOCODSS.

MIMOCODSS, besides being another acronym in the ever lengthening list of acronyms and buzzwords, stands for <u>M</u>ulti-<u>I</u>nput, <u>M</u>ulti-<u>O</u>utput, <u>C</u>ontrollable and <u>O</u>bservable <u>D</u>ecision <u>S</u>upport <u>S</u>ystem. It is essentially an adaptation of the MIMOCOS model of control systems engineering used for the design of a management information and decision support system for a given business process. It is an enterprise wide solution which seamlessly integrates all heterogeneous legacy systems, be they stand alone sub-systems or on-line sub-systems or a combination of the two. To those enamoured by the buzzword ERP, MIMOCODSS can be termed as a home-grown, tailor-made ERP.

As already discussed, any business process can be broken up into its constituent sub-processes. Each of these can be uniquely defined in terms of its inputs and outputs and can be represented by a block diagram. Once the causal relationship of a process or sub-process is known, its integration with other compatible processes or sub-processes becomes as simple a task as rearranging your kid's Lego building blocks. For example, let us consider a typical business process which can be represented by a block diagram as shown in Figure 9.5.

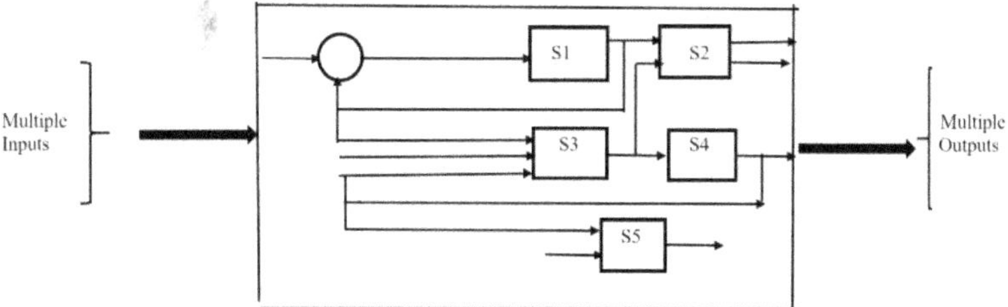

Figure 9.5

This business process is composed of five sub-processes as shown, with each sub-process having well defined inputs and outputs . Consider a situation where, due to some geo-political and/or technological changes, the business environment has also changed, demanding structural modifications to the business process such as deletion of sub-process S5 and introduction of a new sub-process S6 with defined inputs and outputs, so as to remain competitive. In such a case the MIMOCOS modelling methodology makes the task of business process re-engineering quite simple, as all that one needs to do is remove the sub-process block S5 altogether from the block diagram of Figure 9.5 and insert sub-process block S6. The new re-engineered business process will then appear as shown in Figure 9.6..

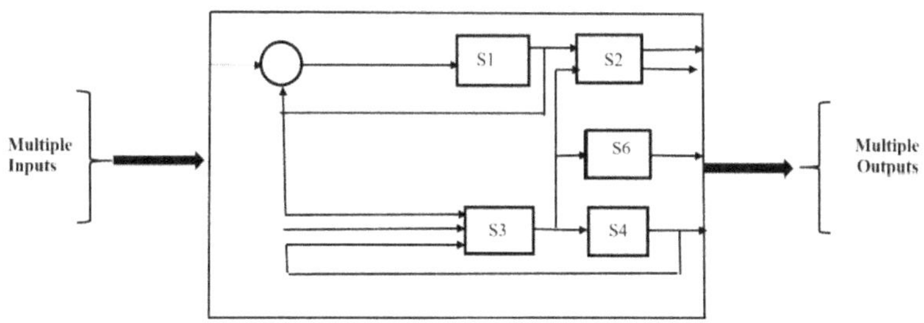

Figure 9.6

Hence a large legacy system or business process comprising a number of smaller legacy systems, each of which can be uniquely defined in terms of its inputs and outputs, lends itself well for analysis and synthesis/integration using the MIMOCOS modelling methodology.

After re-engineering the business process using the MIMOCOS methodology, all that remains to be done to convert it into a MIMOCODSS, is to automate all the integrated sub-processes. This task can be accomplished by first drawing up the System Requirements Specifications (SRS) for each sub-process block, then selecting a suitable database like ORACLE and an appropriate front-end like VISUAL BASIC and finally coding and testing followed by deployment of the modules.

As explained earlier, corporate transformation involves business process re-engineering and automation of the re-engineered business process. The MIMOCOS model gives us the methodology to accomplish these tasks in a simple and straightforward manner.

10

IMPLEMENTATION OF MIMOCODSS-
Case Study

10.1 <u>Introduction</u>

To demonstrate how, in real life, MIMOCOS model has been used to develop a Management Information and Decision Support System called MIMOCODSS, an example in the form of a case study is presented here. MIMOCODSS is a seamlessly integrated enterprise wide IT solution and therefore can be called an ERP solution of a different kind particularly suitable for a company having a large number of proven legacy systems as shown in the case study. A noteworthy feature of the MIMOCODS system is its flexibility.

10.2 <u>Background</u>

This case pertains to a service organisation involved in the business of transportation of goods by sea across the globe. The organisation had, over a period of time, developed systems and procedures pertaining to its business operations. The systems in use were a mix of manual and automated systems. The automated systems comprised of a combination of batch processing systems, on-line systems and stand-alone systems all of which were tailor-made to suit the operations of the organisation and were, therefore tested and proven systems. In short, the organisation had a wealth of proven legacy systems. What the organisation lacked was a seamlessly integrated enterprise-wide single system running on a common database similar to a standard ERP solution to cater to the information needs of the entire organisation.

10.3 <u>The Standard Approach and Its Drawbacks</u>

In order to have an ERP solution implemented across the organisation in the shortest time possible, based on a study of the business processes conducted and the recommendations made by an independent agency, the organisation opted for the big bang approach of ERP implementation i.e., selection of a standard ERP package and mapping of the entire business process on to it at one go. After spending a considerable amount of time, effort and energy, the big bang approach had to be abandoned for the following reasons:

a) The business process and the sub-processes pertaining to the transportation of goods by sea, were unique and peculiar in nature and, therefore, were difficult to map on to a standard ERP package.

b) The various modules of the standard ERP package were not very flexible for adaptation to the business process.

Figure 10.1.1 shows a standard ERP package solution in the form of a block diagram. In the process approach jargon this ERP package can be considered as a business process comprising seven sub-processes. Each sub-process has multiple inputs and outputs.

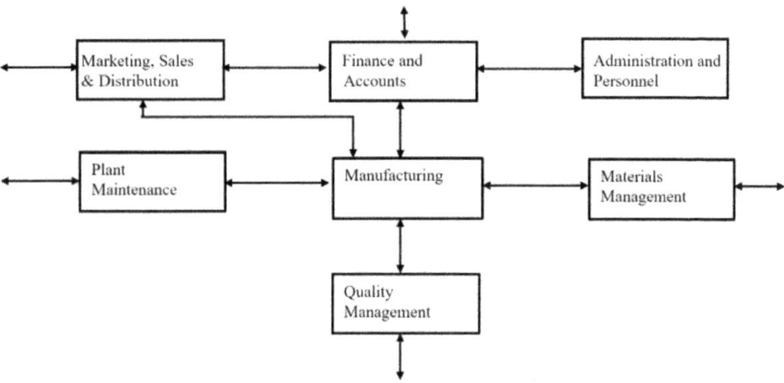

Figure 10.1.1

Now, to provide an enterprise wide IT solution, all the business sub-processes pertaining to the transportation business process had to be fitted into the relevant sub-process blocks of the standard ERP package. As mentioned earlier, because of the uniqueness and peculiar nature of the transportation business, when an attempt was made to map it on to a standard ERP package, the result turned out to be a poor fit as depicted in Figure 10.1.2 which shows some sub-processes fitting properly into the sub-process blocks of the standard ERP and some not fitting into the

blocks at all. At this juncture the choice before the implementing agency of the ERP was either to disregard all those sub-processes that did not fit into the scheme of things or to modify the sub-processes to make them fit into the ERP package. Both these options would have meant heavy compromises from the transportation business point of view and were therefore not acceptable to the organisation. The third option of extensively modifying the ERP modules in order to accommodate all the transportation business processes and sub-processes, was also not an acceptable solution as this would have rendered the ERP package unstable.

<u>Standard ERP Solution for Legacy System</u>

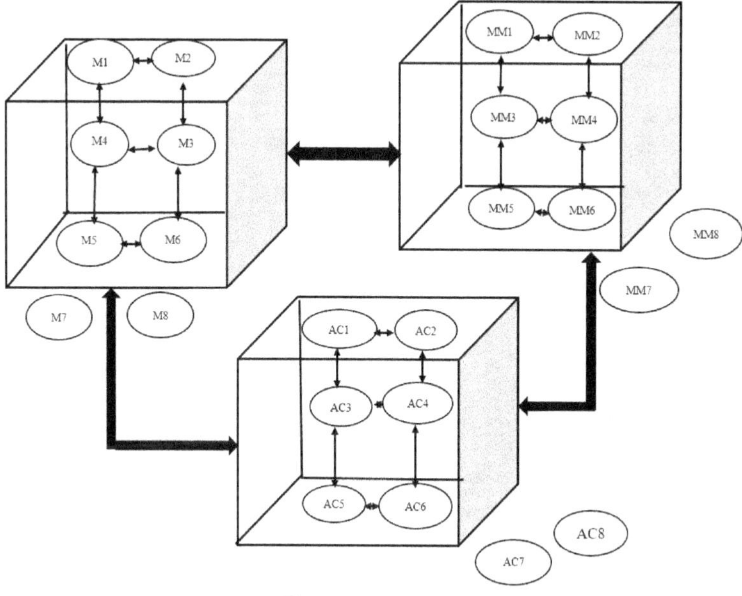

Figure 10.1.2

An ideal ERP solution for a transportation business with scores of legacy systems, should be like the one depicted in Figure 10.1.3 wherein the business process and all its constituent sub-processes are shown to fit snugly into a set of standard ERP modules. But ideal solutions don't exist in real life and therefore, the standard ERP solution formula had to be abandoned in favour of a home-grown solution called MIMOCODSS, which is presented here.

An Ideal ERP Solution for Legacy System

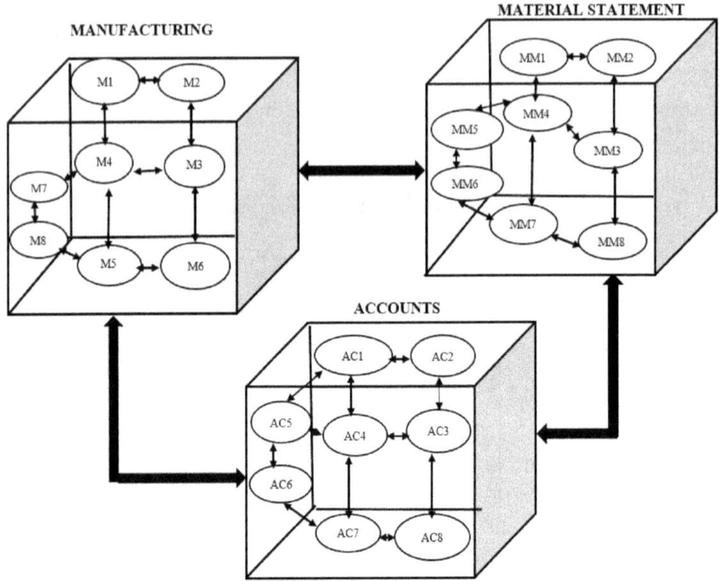

Figure 10.1.3

10.4 The Custom-built Approach

- Taking into account the existence of a large number of legacy systems (over 4000 programs running on COBOL, FOXPRO, VISUAL FOXPRO platforms) designed and developed for the exclusive use of various divisions and departments;

- Recognising the fact that the legacy software have been developed in-house by qualified and experienced software professionals with thorough domain knowledge;

- Giving due regard to the fact that domain knowledge is an absolute must for attempting a corporate transformation which is comprised of business process re-engineering and IT enablement; and

- Realising that all the above conditions exist within the organisation, it was decided to implement MIMOCODSS to serve as an ERP for both management information and decision support.

A step-by-step procedure as detailed below, was adopted to accomplish the task:

1) Based on the flow of information/data from various identified sources to various identified destinations, the MIMOCODS system design was evolved using the MIMOCOS model for this purpose. A block diagram of MIMOCODSS is shown in Figure 10.2.

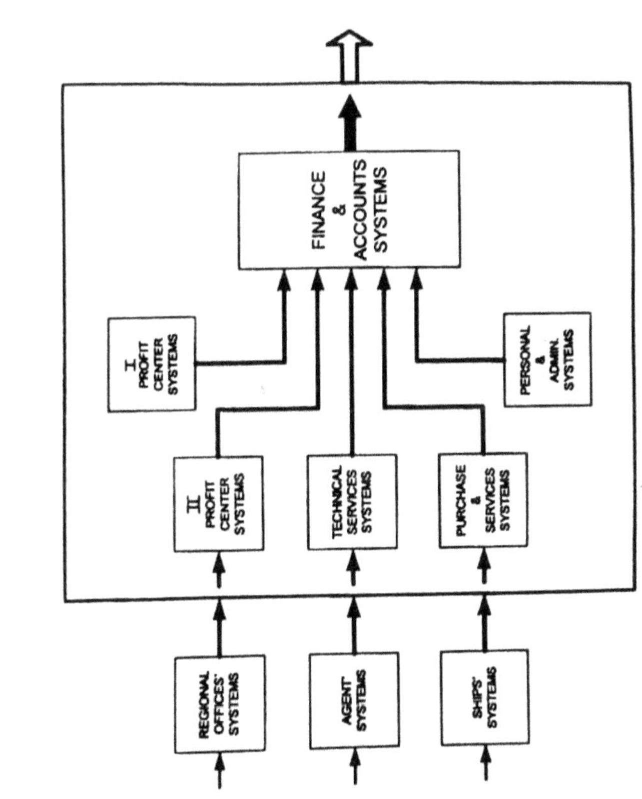

Figure 10.2

2) An inventory of all legacy application software in use was made. For each and every application software, along with the relevant documentation, bubble diagrams were prepared. A sample bubble diagram of a typical legacy sub-system is shown in Figure 10.3. The bubble diagrams served as inputs for creating the block diagrams of the business process and sub-processes for the purposes of analysing and synthesizing the processes.

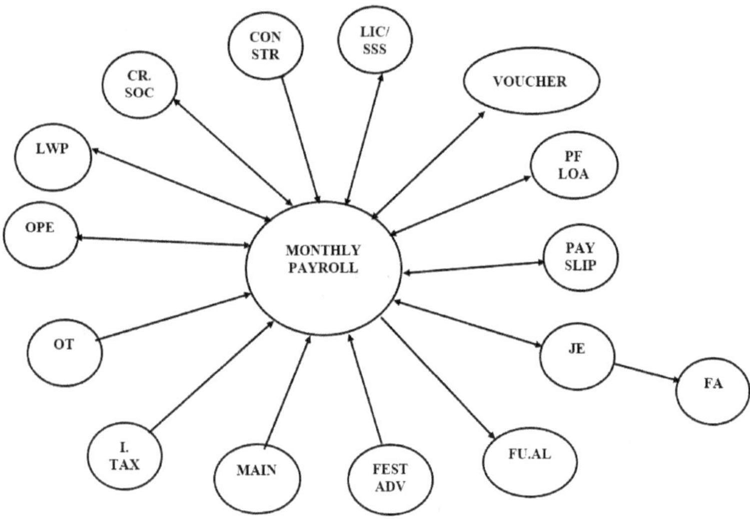

Figure 10.3

3) As a part of the BPR exercise, the block diagram of every business process and sub-process was analysed. Based on the analysis, the unwanted blocks were deleted and new blocks were added to meet the new System Requirements Specifications (SRS), thereby completing the exercise of BP synthesis. Thereafter all the blocks were logically grouped and interlinked appropriately, to complete the process of integration.

4) Keeping in view the allotted budget, licencing costs, annual maintenance cost, upgrade fees and other cost bearing items, as well as security related concerns, the UNIX Operating System and

ORACLE database along with Developer 2000 as front end was decided upon as the platform for MIMOCODSS.

5) Having thus completed the process of BPR which comprised of BP analysis, BP synthesis as well as system integration and also having selected the right technology and tools (platform, database, front end etc.) for deploying the modules, the job of programming/coding and testing were taken up and completed. Some typical examples of BP analysis, BP synthesis and system integration are shown in Figures 10.3 ,10.4, and 10.5.

Figure 10.3 depicts the bubble diagram of a legacy payroll sub-system which was required to be re-engineered to meet the changed specifications of the business process. This bubble diagram was converted to a block diagram of a legacy payroll sub-system as shown in Figure 10.4 for the purpose of analysis. Based on the analysis of the sub-system, it was found that sub-process block marked FU-AL being redundant, was to be deleted and two new sub-process blocks CB and KOL.PAYROLL were to be incorporated to meet the new requirements of the business process. Figure 10.5 depicts the re-engineered payroll sub-system. This sub-system was then incorporated in the Finance and Accounts Systems block shown in Figure 10.2. On similar lines other sub-systems were re-engineered and incorporated in the various main system blocks such as I Profit Centre Systems, II Profit Centre Systems, Technical Services Systems, Purchase and Services Systems and Personal and Administration Systems shown in Figure 10.2. Subsequently, integration of the main system blocks was carried out.

Figure 10.6 shows the block diagram of MIMOCODSS after incorporation and integration of various systems and sub-systems. The block diagram of MIMOCODSS shown here is representative in nature as it is meant for the purpose of illustration, only. The MIMOCODSS in real life has over seventy sub-systems which exhaustively covers all the areas of operation of the organisation.

BLOCK DIAGRAM OF LEGACY PAYROLL SUB- SYSTEM

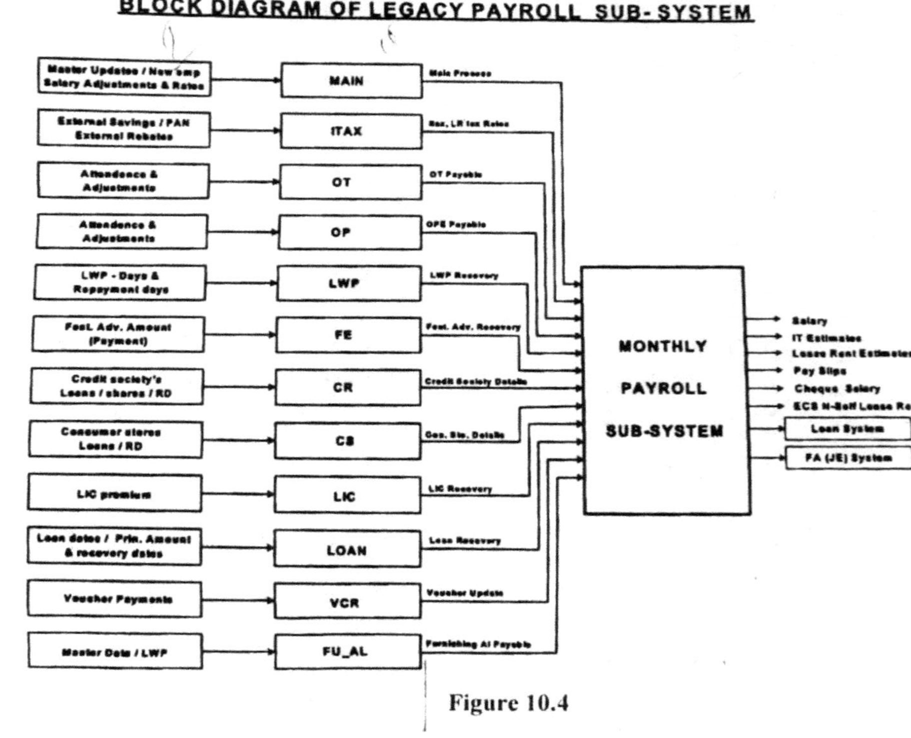

Figure 10.4

BLOCK DIAGRAM OF RE-ENGINEERED PAYROLL SUB-SYSTEM

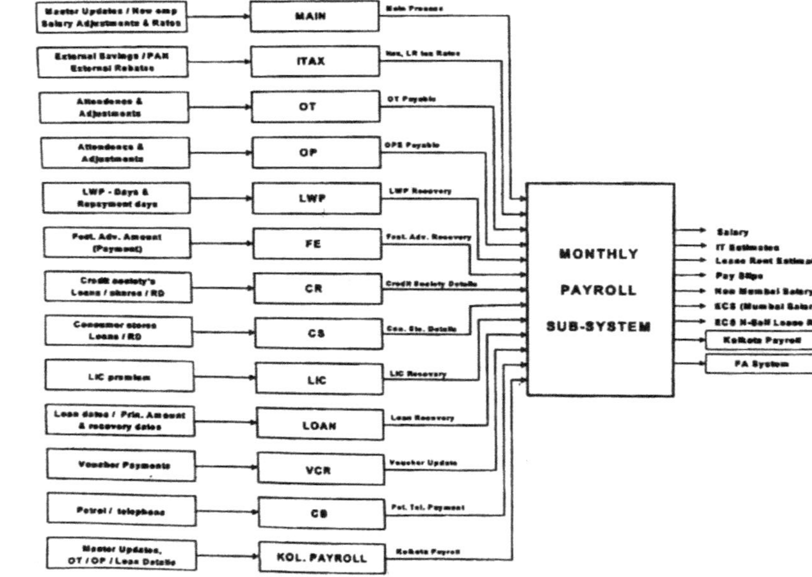

Figure 10.5

MIMOCODSS

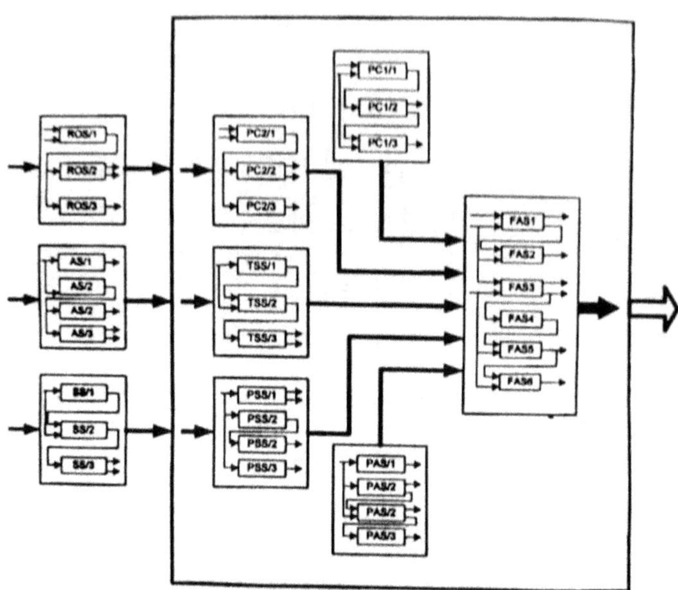

Figure 10.6

11

ERP, Artificial Intelligence and Related Case Studies

11.1 Introduction

Technologies in the current situation have paved the way for new techniques of functioning with succession of new technologies becoming the primary drivers of the new norm.

While Artificial Intelligence(AI) and Machine Learning(ML) inspired systems are being deployed in almost every field of activity, including health care,education,finance,commerce,agriculture,but most of the individuals and industries are not yet familiar with the concept of AI/ML and Data Science. There is,however, a realisation that AI/ML has considerable potential for altering processes, but it is yet not clear as to how AI/ML and related techniques could be deployed in businesses in varied sectors.

It is human nature to try to know about the future so that preemptive action,if necessary, can be planned in advance for ones betterment.Just as people would like to go through the astrological predictions daily to know what the future holds for them, businessmen and entrepreneurs would also like to know how their respective businesses would fare in the future. In the latter case, however, predictions are not based on planetary positions and their movements but on modern scientific methods. In this chapter case studies / examples from the business world are presented that are based on AI/ML and other related techniques for the prediction of the future trends of businesses.

11.2 Artificial Intelligence and Machine Learning

Artificial Intelligence(AI) refers to the simulation of human intelligence in machines that are programmed to think like humans and mimic their actions. The term is applied to any machine that exhibits traits associated with a human mind such as learning and problem- solving.

AI is continuously evolving to benefit many different industries.The application of AI is endless. AI as a technology can be applied to many different sectors and industries. AI has applications in accounts, banking and finance.AI is also being applied to streamline businesses in order to make the conduct of business easier.

The terms Artificial Intelligence and Machine Learning are being used interchangeably but there is a distinct difference between the two. Artificial Intelligence is a bigger concept to create intelligent machines that can simulate human thinking capability and behaviour,while Machine Learning is an application or subset of Artificial Intelligence that allows machines to learn from past data without being programmed,explicitly.Thus AI can be thought of as the mother and ML its child. In this chapter the term ML will be used and simple examples of AI/ML and allied techniques as applied to some business processes, will be illustrated.

Machine Learning(ML) are of three types,namely, Supervised Learning,Unsupervised Learning and Reinforcement Learning.

Supervised learning is a machine learning algorithm that learns from sets of labelled data or examples from the past and predicts or gives decision based on new sets of data or examples. Labelled data are data that have features denoted by the variables X and prediction or decision denoted by the variables Y.

Unsupervised learning is a machine learning algorithm that looks for previously undetected patterns in unlabelled data set or examples denoted by the variables X alone and with no pre-existing labels i.e.Y.

Reinforcement learning is a machine learning algorithm that pertains to how an agent ought to take actions in an environment in order to maximize the notion of cumulative reward.

The languages that AI and ML understand are Mathematics and Statistics.However, in order to ensure that the examples of AI/ML presented here are accessable to every reader, the mathematical and statistical contents are kept to the minimum. For the purpose of illustration,case studies/examples pertaining to the supervised learning type of ML algorithm are presented in this work, as exhaustive treatment of all the aspects of AI/ML is beyond the scope of this book.

11.3 <u>Application of Machine Learning to Ships Sale and Purchase Process.</u>

Annually, the ships sale and purchase business is valued at millions of dollars. When a new entrepreneur desires to venture into the business of running ships,commercially, he normally considers prudent to purchase a second hand vessel as against a new ship, in order to keep the risk of the venture to the minimum. The second hand market presents a number of options with a variety of features and varying costs. Here, AI/ML can help the entrepreneur to make an informed choice. In the following paragraphs a Machine Learning algorithm is presented under supervised learning for ships sale and purchase process, using the Linear Regression Model.

Hypothesis, represented by the symbol h_θ (x) is the term used in ML to represent the formula that is used for prediction.

$$h_\theta(x) = \theta_0 + \theta_1 x_1 + \theta_2 x_2 + \theta_3 x_3 + \ldots + \theta_n \qquad (11.1)$$

In the above formula $\theta_1, \theta_2 \ldots \theta_n$ are called parameters or weightages and $x_1, x_2 \ldots x_n$ are termed as features such as the deadweight,age, TC hire, scrap price, etc of the ship.

The Cost Function which is represented by the symbol $J(\theta)$ whose minimization determines the numerical values for the parameters or weightages,namely,$\theta_1, \theta_2 \ldots \theta_n$ is given by the following expression:

$$J(\theta) = \frac{1}{2m} \sum_{i=1}^{m} (h_\theta(x^{(i)}) - y^{(i)})^2 + \frac{\lambda}{2m} \sum_{j=i}^{n} \theta_j^2 \qquad (11.2)$$

In the above expression "m" is the number of training examples or training data sets, "n" is the number of parameters or weightages and "λ" is the Regularization parameter.

For the determination of θ's the following two methods are available:

1) The Gradient Descent Algorithm Method:

This is an iterative method in which the procedure is repeatedly applied until convergence:

Repeat until convergence:

$$\left\{ \theta_j := \theta_j - \alpha \frac{\partial}{\partial \theta_j} J(\theta) \text{ (for } j = 0 \ldots n) \right\} \qquad (11.3)$$

2)Normal Equation Method:

In the normal equation method for determining the values of θ's the following equation is used:

$$\Theta = (X^T X)^{-1} X^T y, \qquad\qquad (11.4)$$

Where,

$$\Theta = \begin{bmatrix} \theta_0 \\ \theta_1 \\ . \\ . \\ \theta_n \end{bmatrix}, X^{(i)} = \begin{bmatrix} x_0^{(i)} \\ x_2^{(i)} \\ . \\ . \\ x_n^{(i)} \end{bmatrix} \in R^{n+1}, X = \begin{bmatrix} 1 & x_1^{(1)} & x_2^{(1)} & .... & x_n^{(1)} \\ 1 & x_1^{(2)} & x_2^{(2)} & .... & x_n^{(2)} \\ . & . & . & . & . \\ . & . & . & . & . \\ 1 & x_1^{(m)} & x_2^{(m)} & .... & x_n^{(m)} \end{bmatrix} \text{ and } y^{(i)} = \begin{bmatrix} y^{(1)} \\ y^{(2)} \\ . \\ . \\ y^{(m)} \end{bmatrix}$$

A COMPARISION OF THE METHODS

GRADIENT DESCENT METHOD	NORMAL EQUATION METHOD
1)Need to choose the learning rate "α".	1)No need to choose the learning rate "α".
2)Features scaling necessary.	2)Features scaling not required.
3)Needs many iterations.	3)No need for iterations.
4)Works very well even when the number of features "n" is very large.	4)Need to compute $(X^T X)^{-1}$ 5)The computing process becomes slow when the number of features "n" is very large.

11.4 <u>Case Studies</u>

In the case studies presented here two sets of data of ships are considered. The number of features "n" of the ship considered for the computation are six, namely,ship's dead weight,ship's age, merit rating of the ship yard where the ship was built,ship's special survey/dry dock validity period,TC hire and ship's current scrap price.As this number is small the normal equation method for the computation of the parameters or weightages "θ" is suitable and appropriate.The block diagram cum data flow diagram for this case study is shown Figure 11.1.

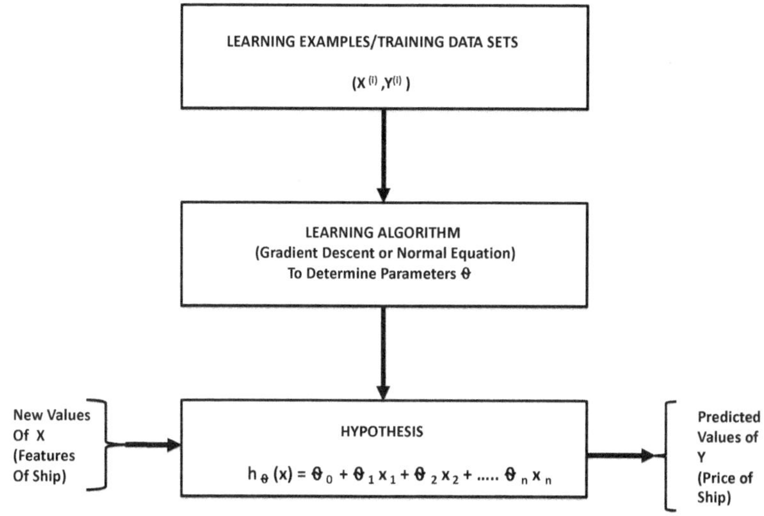

$$h_\theta(x) = \theta_0 + \theta_1 x_1 + \theta_2 x_2 + \dots \theta_n x_n$$

Figure 11.1

11.4.1 <u>Case 1- Ships Sale Data for Six Ships</u>

Ship Type	Ship Name	Dead Weight Dwt	Ship's Age (Years)	Yard Rating (Scale 1-5)	SS/DD Validity (Months)	TC Hire ($)	Scrap Price ($/Lwt)	Price Sold (Million $)
Bulker	MIMI SELMER	55711	15	5	3	10500	315	7.5
Bulker	NIKKEI VERDI	51658	9	5	15	10500	315	10.5
Bulker	PEGASUS OCEAN	34512	5	5	3	7500	315	14
Bulker	GRACEFUL MADONNA	180242	10	5	53	23000	310	20.8
Bulker	MEDI LAUSANNE	83002	14	5	4	11500	310	9.7
Bulker	AP REVELIN	38795	4	3	6	7750	295	13

Table 11.1

In order to use the normal equation for determining the values of θs , the ships data given in the above Table 11.1 needs to be cast in an appropriate format as follows:

Bias X_0	Dead weight X_1	Ship's Age (Years) X_2	Ship Yard Rating (Scale 1-5) X_3	SS/DD Validity (Months) X_4	TC Hire (in \$) X_5	Scrap Price (\$/Lwt) X_6	Price Sold (Million \$) y
1	55711	15	5	3	10500	315	7.5
1	51658	9	5	15	10500	315	10.5
1	34512	5	5	3	7500	315	14
1	180242	10	5	53	23000	310	20.8
1	83002	14	5	4	11500	310	9.7
1	38795	4	3	6	7750	295	13

Table 11.2

The data from the above Table 11.2 needs to be cast in a Matrix form as shown below:

$$X(Features) = \begin{bmatrix} 1 & 55711 & -15 & 5 & 3 & 315 & 10500 \\ 1 & 51658 & -9 & 5 & 15 & 315 & 10500 \\ 1 & 34512 & -5 & 5 & 3 & 315 & 7500 \\ 1 & 180242 & -10 & 5 & 53 & 310 & 23000 \\ 1 & 83002 & -14 & 5 & 4 & 310 & 11500 \\ 1 & 38795 & -4 & 3 & 6 & 295 & 7750 \end{bmatrix} \tag{11.5}$$

$$y(Price) = \begin{bmatrix} 7.5 \\ 10.5 \\ 14 \\ 20.8 \\ 9.7 \\ 13 \end{bmatrix} \tag{11.6}$$

The Normal Equation to find parameters is $\Theta = (X^T X)^{-1} X^T$

$$\tag{11.7}$$

The solution to Equation (11.7) yields:

$\theta_0 = -56.4$, $\theta_1 = -0.000134$, $\theta_2 = 1.38$, $\theta_3 = 2.87$, $\theta_4 = -0.493$, $\theta_5 = 0.038$, $\theta_6 = 0.0035$.

Substitution of the above values of θs in Equation (1) gives rise to the hypothesis:

$$h_\theta(x) = -56.4 - 0.000134x_1 + 1.38x_2 + 2.87x_3 - 0.493x_4 + 0.038x_5 + 0.0035x_6 \tag{11.8}$$

Insertion of a new set of desirable features(x) of the ship that the prospective buyer wants to acquire, in Equation (11.8) will give the predicted price of the ship.

11.4.2 <u>Case 2-Ships Sale Data for Ten Ships</u>

Ship Type	Ship Name	Dead Weight Dwt	Ship's Age (Years)	Yard Rating (Scale1-5)	SS/DD Validity (Months)	TC Hire ($)	Scrap Price ($/Lwt)	Price Sold (Million$)
Bulker	MIMI SELMER	55711	15	5	3	10500	315	7.5
Bulker	NIKKEI VERDI	51658	9	5	15	10500	315	10.5
Bulker	PEGASUS OCEAN	34512	5	5	3	7500	315	14
Bulker	GRACEFUL MADONNA	180242	10	5	53	23000	310	20.8
Bulker	MEDI LAUSANNE	83002	14	5	4	11500	310	9.7
Bulker	AP REVELIN	38795	4	3	6	7750	295	13
Tanker	AGILITY	44970	23	4	22	325	13500	5
Tanker	HRA	320105	9	4	15	325	40000	48
Tanker	PETROLIMEX 06	35758	24	5	14	325	7500	3
Tanker	HIGH PROGRESS	51303	15	4	-1	320	14500	12.5

Table 11.3

Repeating the same procedure followed for Case 1, the data from the above Table 11.3 when cast in the Matrix form would appear as shown below:

$$
X(Features) =
\begin{bmatrix}
1 & 55711 & -15 & 5 & 3 & 315 & 10500 \\
1 & 51658 & -9 & 5 & 15 & 315 & 10500 \\
1 & 34512 & -5 & 5 & 3 & 315 & 7500 \\
1 & 180242 & -10 & 5 & 53 & 310 & 23000 \\
1 & 83002 & -14 & 5 & 4 & 310 & 11500 \\
1 & 38795 & -4 & 3 & 6 & 295 & 7750 \\
1 & 44970 & -23 & 4 & 22 & 325 & 13500 \\
1 & 320105 & -9 & 4 & 16 & 325 & 40000 \\
1 & 35758 & -24 & 5 & 14 & 325 & 7500 \\
1 & 51303 & -15 & 4 & -1 & 320 & 14500
\end{bmatrix}
\quad \text{and } y =
\begin{bmatrix}
7.5 \\ 10.5 \\ 14 \\ 20.8 \\ 9.7 \\ 13 \\ 5 \\ 48 \\ 3 \\ 12.5
\end{bmatrix}
$$

On solving the normal equation $\theta = (X^{1}X)^{-1}X^{T}y$, the following values for θs are obtained:

$\theta_0 = -109, \theta_1 = 0.000148, \theta_2 = 0.803, \theta_3 = -3.59, \theta_4 = -0.0584, \theta_5 = 0.453, \theta_6 = -.000372$

A comparision of the values of θs obtained in the case of six ships and ten ships respectively, is given in the following Table 11.4:

PARAMETERS θ FOR SIX SHIPS	PARAMETERS θ FOR TEN SHIPS
$\theta_0 = -56.4$	$\theta_0 = -109$
$\theta_1 = -0.000134$	$\theta_1 = 0.000148$
$\theta_2 = 1.38$	$\theta_2 = 0.803$
$\theta_3 = 2.87$	$\theta_3 = -3.59$
$\theta_4 = -0.493$	$\theta_4 = -0.0584$
$\theta_5 = 0.038$	$\theta_5 = 0.453$
$\theta_6 = 0.0035$	$\theta_6 = -0.000372$

Table 11.4

From the above Table 11.4 it is evident that the values of θs vary widely thus conveying the fact that the price of the ship predicted by the hypothesis $h_\theta(x)$, based on these values of θs, is not dependable. The principal reason for this is that the learning algorithm used for determining the values of θs is not sufficiently trained. This is because the number of training data sets or examples supplied for training the algorithm was very small.For making the algorithm sufficiently learned in order to enable the hypothesis to make a reasonably acceptable prediction of ship's price, the minimum number of training data sets(ships' past sale & purchase data) required is 800. On supplying 800 past data sets to the learning algorithm, the values of the parameters θ generated by the algorithm will converge to assume unique values that will enable the hypothesis $h_\theta(x)$ to predict the right price when a new set of ship's features are given as inputs to it.Further, it is a standard practice in an AI/ ML project to test the algorithm with another 200 additional test data sets followed by a validation process using for the purpose yet another 200 data sets to complete the project, satisfactorily

In the case studies presented here all the features of the ships used in the hypothesis are assumed to be linear functions. However, there can be instances where the features are quadratic or cubic or even polynomial in nature thus leading to problems of over fitting. Resolution of such problems can be achieved by resorting to regularization using the regularization parameter λ.

11.5 <u>Monte Carlo Simulation</u>

Monte Carlo simulation or Monte Carlo experiments, are a broad class of computational algorithms that rely on repeated random sampling to obtain numerical results. The idea underlining the Monte Carlo method is to use randomness to solve problems that might be deterministic in nature. This method is widely used in solving problems in Physical Sciences, Engineering, ArtificialIntelligence, Finance and Business. Uses of Monte Carlo methods require large amounts of random numbers, and it was the use of random numbers that spurred the development of pseudorandom number generators.

In this section a simple case of predicting the future demand for a particular product for a given period of time, using the past data and the Monte Carlo method of simulation, is being presented.

A step by step procedure for Monte Carlo simulation method is given below:

1) Set up a probability distribution for the variables to be analyzed.

2) Build a cumulative probability distribution for each random variable.

3) Generate random numbers and then assign an appropriate set of random numbers to represent a range of values for each random variable.

4) Conduct the simulation experiment using random sampling.

5) Repeat step number 4 until the required number of simulation runs has been generated.

6) Design and implement a course of action and maintain control.

A block diagram cum data flow diagram for the simulation experiment is shown in Figure 11.2.

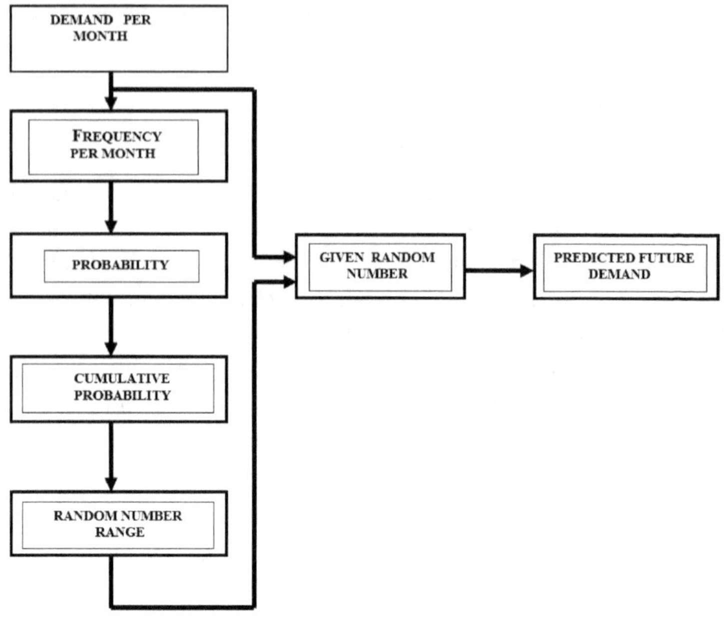

Figure 11.2

11.5.1 <u>Case Study</u>

A company manufactures a product for which the demand per month (in 100 units) for the past six(6) months was as follows:

Demand/Month (in 100s)	0	5	10	20	30	40
Number of Months	2	11	8	21	5	3

Table 11.5

Using the following sequence of random numbers, simulate the demand for the next 10 months.Also predict the average demand:

83,35,57,74,73,23,13,90,52,35

Demand / Month (in 100s)	Frequency (No.of Months) F	Probability $F / \sum F$	Cumulative Probability	Random Number Range
0	2	0.04	0.04	00-03
5	11	0.22	0.26	04-25
10	8	0.16	0.42	26-41
15	21	0.42	0.84	42-83
20	5	0.10	0.94	84-93
25	3	0.06	1.0	94-99
	$\sum F = 50$	$\sum$Probability $= 1$		

Table 11.6

Using the data in Table 11.6, the simulated demand for the next ten months is as follows:

Month	Random Number	Range of Random Number	Simulated Demand (in units of 100)
1	83	42-83	20
2	35	26-41	10
3	57	42-83	20
4	74	42-83	20
5	73	42-83	20
6	23	04-25	05
7	13	04-25	05
8	90	84-93	30

9	52	42-83	20
10	35	26-41	10
			$\Sigma = 160$

Table 11.7

From the above Table 11.7 the predicted total demand for the next ten months

Is 160x100=16000 units,

The projected average demand for the next ten months
= 160 X 100 / 10 = 1600 units per month.

This case is a typical example of a commercial application of Monte Carlo Simulation technique for production or inventory management.

11.6 **Markov Chain and Process**

By definition, a Markov chain is a discrete-time process for which the future behaviour,given the past and the present,only depends on the present and not on the past.A Markov process, on the otherhand,is the continuous-time version of a Markov chain.

Markov chain model can be used to predict the future state of a business,given its present state and the transition probability. This concept can best be illustrated by the following example:

11.6.1 **Case Study.**

A small town with a population of 1000 has three departmental stores A,B and C where the inhabitants of the town do their weekly shopping. On a given week 400 people go for their weekly shopping to store A,240 people go to store B and 360 people go to store C. But in the following week some people will not necessarily go back to the same store for some reason. In such an event what could happen in the following week is, 80% of the shoppers will go back to store A, 70% will go back to store B and 60% will go back to store C. Out of those who do not go back to store A, 10% will go to store B and 10% to store C. In the case of store B, out of the 30% that don't go back to B,20% will go to store A and the remaining 10% head to store C. As for store C, out of the 40% that move away from it, 10% will go to store A and 30% to store B. The distribution of 1000 shoppers among the departmental stores A,B and C and the probabilities of migration of shoppers from stores A,B and C are shown in Figure 11.3.

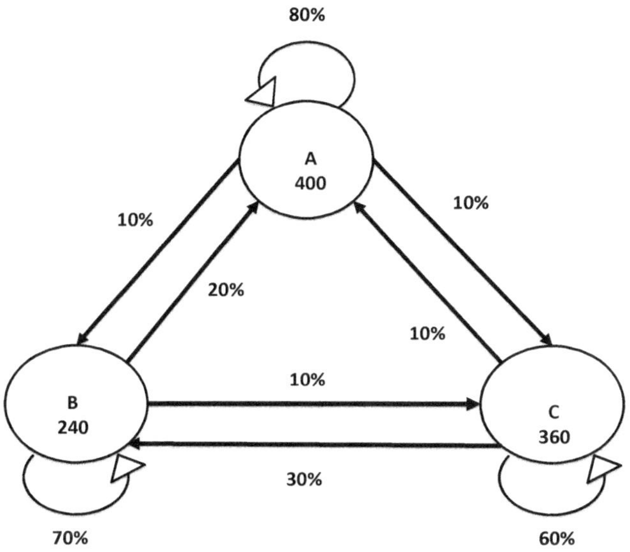

Figure 11.3

In such a scenario, the concerned store owners would like to know what will be the number of shoppers going to stores A,B and C in the following week, if the probability of migration of shoppers as shown in the Markov model diagram Figure 11.3 remains the same. Markov Chain enables predicition of customer bases of stores A,B and C,respectively, over a period of time.

The Markov chain can be represented by the following expression:

[Future State Matrix X_1] = [Transition Probability Matrix P] [Initial State Matrix X_0]   (11.9)

In other words, $X_1 = P * X_0$ (1)   (11.10)

where X_0 is the initial state, X_1 is the state in the following week and

P is the transition probability matrix

Given that $X_1 = \begin{bmatrix} A_1 \\ B_1 \\ C_1 \end{bmatrix}$, $P = \begin{bmatrix} 0.8 & 0.2 & 0.1 \\ 0.1 & 0.7 & 0.3 \\ 0.1 & 0.1 & 0.6 \end{bmatrix}$, $X_0 = \begin{bmatrix} A = \dfrac{400}{1000} = 0.40 \\ B = \dfrac{240}{1000} = 0.24 \\ C = \dfrac{360}{1000} = 0.36 \end{bmatrix}$

By substituting the above values of P and X_0 in equation (11.10). We get,

$$[X_1] = \begin{bmatrix} A_1 \\ B_1 \\ C_1 \end{bmatrix} = \begin{bmatrix} 0.8 & 0.2 & 0.1 \\ 0.1 & 0.7 & 0.3 \\ 0.1 & 0.1 & 0.6 \end{bmatrix}\begin{bmatrix} 0.4 \\ 0.24 \\ 0.36 \end{bmatrix} = \begin{bmatrix} (0.8)*(0.4)+(0.2)*(0.24)+(0.1)*(0.36) \\ (0.1)*(0.4)+(0.7)*(0.24)+(0.3)*(0.36) \\ (0.1)*(0.4)+(0.1)*(0.24)+(0.6)*(0.36) \end{bmatrix} = \begin{bmatrix} 0.404 \\ 0.316 \\ 0.280 \end{bmatrix}$$

Therefore, after one week, out of a population of 1000 shoppers, the number of shoppers going to store A will be $A_1 = 0.404*1000 = 404$,

the number of shoppers going to store B will be $B_1 = 0.316*1000 = 316$ and the number of shoppers going to store C will be $C_1 = 0.280*1000 = 280$ as depicted in Figure 11.4.

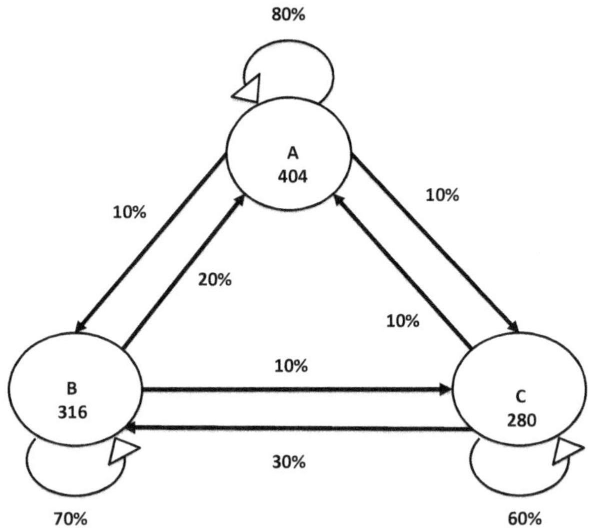

Figure 11.4

Upon seeing the migration of shoppers after one week, the owners of the three departmental stores will now be eager to know what will be their respective customer base in each of the following weeks and when will these numbers stabilize, if the transition probability remains the same throughout.

The Markov chain expression for the future states is as follows:

[Future State Matris X_n] = [Transition Probability Matrix P]^n[Initial State Matrix X_0]

In other words, $X_n = P^n * X_0$ $\qquad\qquad\qquad$ (11.11)

where n is the number of weeks after the initial week.

Thus, for the current example, namely,

$$[X_n] = \begin{bmatrix} A_n \\ B_n \\ C_n \end{bmatrix} = \begin{bmatrix} 0.8 & 0.2 & 0.1 \\ 0.1 & 0.7 & 0.3 \\ 0.1 & 0.1 & 0.6 \end{bmatrix}^n \begin{bmatrix} 0.40 \\ 0.24 \\ 0.36 \end{bmatrix} \qquad (11.12)$$

In the above equation(11.12), if we substitute n = 7 and n = 8, respectively, then we get,

$$[X_7] = \begin{bmatrix} A_7 \\ B_7 \\ C_7 \end{bmatrix} = \begin{bmatrix} 0.8 & 0.2 & 0.1 \\ 0.1 & 0.7 & 0.3 \\ 0.1 & 0.1 & 0.6 \end{bmatrix}^7 \begin{bmatrix} 0.40 \\ 0.24 \\ 0.36 \end{bmatrix} = \begin{bmatrix} 0.45 \\ 0.35 \\ 0.20 \end{bmatrix} \qquad (11.13)$$

$$\text{and } [X_8] = \begin{bmatrix} A_8 \\ B_8 \\ C_8 \end{bmatrix} = \begin{bmatrix} 0.8 & 0.2 & 0.1 \\ 0.1 & 0.7 & 0.3 \\ 0.1 & 0.1 & 0.6 \end{bmatrix}^8 \begin{bmatrix} 0.40 \\ 0.24 \\ 0.20 \end{bmatrix} = \begin{bmatrix} 0.45 \\ 0.35 \\ 0.2 \end{bmatrix} \qquad (11.14)$$

On examination of the above equations (11.13) and (11.14) it can be observed that the final values of [X_7] and [X_8] are identical indicating that the Markov chain has stabilized resulting in a stable state distribution matrix. The stable state distribution matrix is conventionally represented by the symbol $\overline{X}$. From the stable state distribution matrix the final distribution of shoppers between the three departmental stores A,B and C can be computed as follows:

Shoppers at store A = 0.45*1000 = 450, shoppers at store B = 0.35*1000 = 350 and shoppers at store C = 0.2*1000 = 200. This redistribution of shoppers is shown in Figure 11.5.

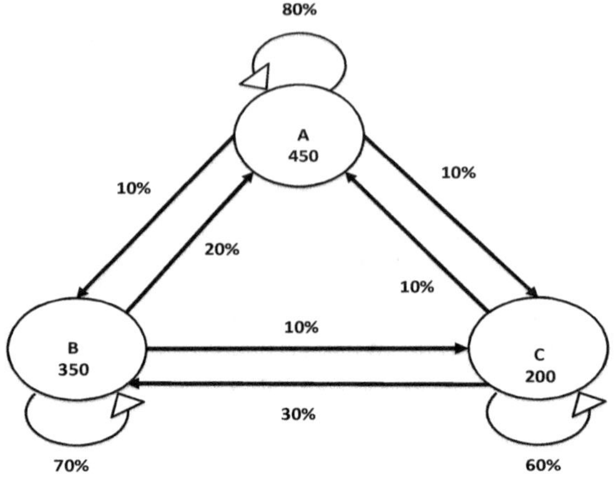

Figure 11.5

Alternative Method to Compute the Stable State

The method outlined above to compute the stable state could be a bit cumbersome. An alternative method to compute the stable state $\overline{X}$, given the transient probability matrix P, is as follows:

From the equations 11.13 and 11.14 we know that $P * \overline{X} = \overline{X}$ (11.15)

Let $\overline{X} = \begin{bmatrix} A \\ B \\ C \end{bmatrix}$, now by substituting the given values for P and $\overline{X}$ in the above equation 11.15, we get,

$$\begin{bmatrix} 0.8 & 0.2 & 0.3 \\ 0.1 & 0.7 & 0.1 \\ 0.1 & 0.1 & 0.6 \end{bmatrix} \begin{bmatrix} A \\ B \\ C \end{bmatrix} = \begin{bmatrix} A \\ B \\ C \end{bmatrix}$$ 11.16

On solving the above matrix equation 11.16, we get the following three simultaneous equations:

$0.8A + 0.2B + 0.1C = A$ 11.17

$0.1A + 0.7B + 0.3C = B$ 11.18

$0.1A + 0.1B + 0.6C = C$ 11.19

It is also known that: $A + B + C = 1$ 11.20

On solving the above set of four simultaneous equations, we get,

A = 9/20 = 0.45, B = 7/20 = 0.35 and C = 4/20 = 0.20

From the computed values of A,B and C the final stable distribution of 1000 shoppers among the departmental stores A,B and C can be computed as follows:

Shoppers at store A = 0.45*1000 = 450, shoppers at store B = 0.35*1000 = 350 and shoppers at store C = 0.20*1000 = 200. Thus, the redistribution of shoppers remains the same as shown in Figure 11.5.

11.7 <u>Application of Systems Approach to Accounts</u>

<u>Objective and Purpose</u>

The objectives and purpose of a business process re-engineering / enterprise resource planning project are:

(i) To Analyse the Process/Sub-Processes/Tasks , and if necessary, modify the Inputs and Business Rules so as to obtain the desired Outputs.

(ii) To Synthesize the various Sub- Processes/ Tasks, then integrate the Sub -Processes to form the Main Process and finally digitalize the Main Process.

In the systems approach, **as described in Chapter 9**, a business process is made of sub-processes and each sub-process in turn, is made up of tasks. The business rule transforms the inputs to the task into appropriate outputs. In the cases described below, each transaction can be considered as one of the tasks pertaining to, for example, the finance module of a typical ERP System.

In the case studies presented below, the common golden rules of accounting namely, Personal account (Debit the receiver/ Credit the giver), Real account (Debit What comes in/ Credit what goes out) And Nominal account (Debit all expenses and losses / Credit all Incomes and Gains) become the business rules. The business rules could be in the form of a mathematical expression or a formula or plain text. In the case studies presented here the business rules are, by and large, in the form of text. In the systems approach, as a convention, thick arrows are used to indicate multiple inputs or outputs and thin arrows are used to indicate a single input or output.

11.7.1 <u>Receivables and Payables</u>

Accounts receivable is the amount owed to a company when the company provides goods and/or services on credit. Accounts receivable is also called as Trade Receivable. The amount that the company is owed is recorded in its general ledger account entitled Accounts Receivable. The unpaid balance in this account is reported as part of the Current assets listed on the Company's balance sheet.

Accounts Payable is the amount of liability of the company or business towards its suppliers when the suppliers provide goods and/or services on credit. Accounts Payable is also called as Trade Payable. The amount of liability of the company is recorded in its general ledger account entitled Accounts Payable. The unpaid balance on this account is reported as a part of Current Liabilities on the Company's Balance sheet.

Case: 1

i) <u>At the time of recording a credit sale and billing the customer</u>

Accounts Receivable (Debtors) a/c Dr.   xxx

       To Sales (On Credit)   xxx

On 21st September 2019, Ram sold goods worth Rs 7000 to Shyam on credit.

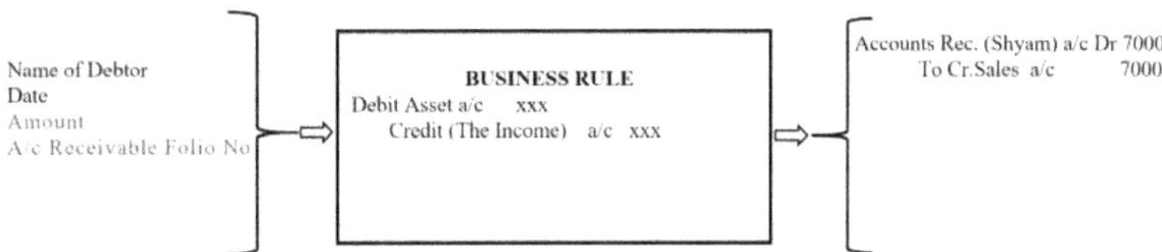

Ram raised a Bill of exchange of Rs 7000 on Shyam via folio number FRBXXX90. According to Systems Approach, in this case the transaction can be represented as follows:

Bills Receivable a/c Dr.   xxx

  To Accounts Receivable(Shyam) a/c   xxx

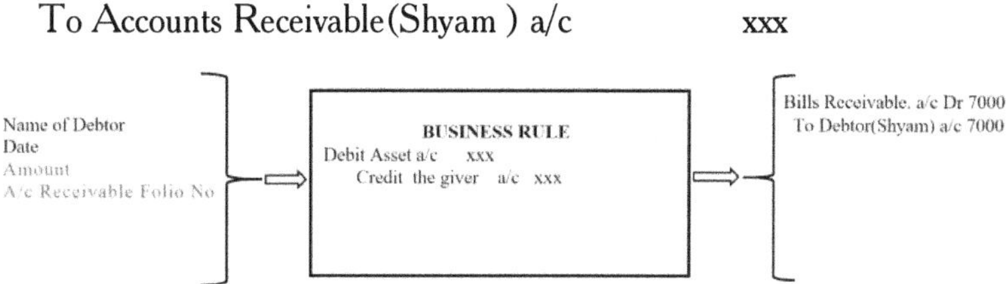

ii) At the time when money is received from customer

Cash/ Bank a/c Dr.   7000

              To Bills Receivables a/c   7000

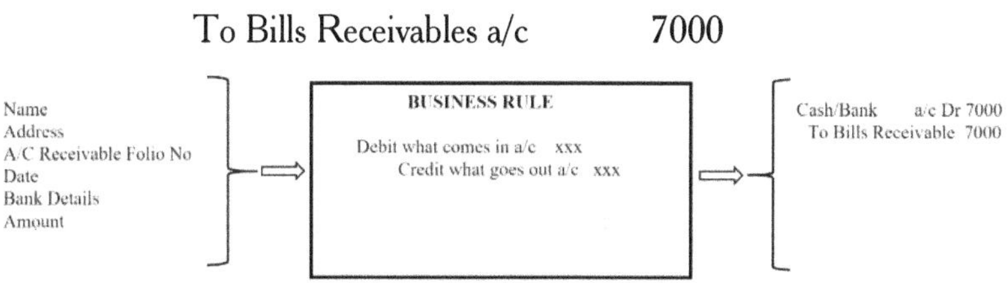

Case 2

<u>Bills Receivable Dishonoured</u>

If the Bills are not settled on the due date, the process is reversed and the amount owed by customer is transferred back to A/c Receivable.

Customer is liable to pay the noting charges and fees paid by business.

Debtors(Shyam) a/c Dr.   7100

        To Bills Receivable   7000

        To Cash   100

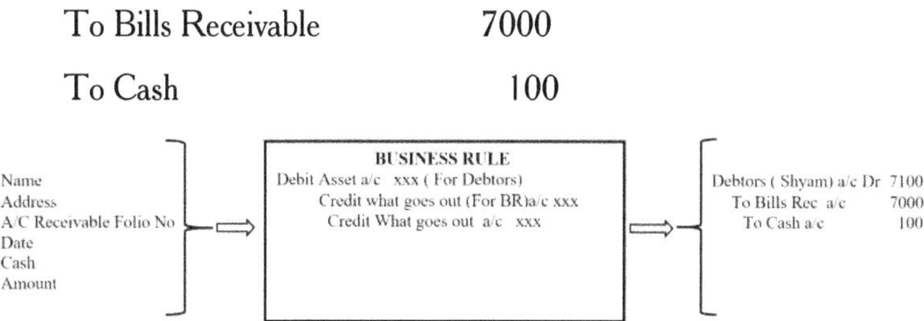

<u>On receipt of dues from Customer</u>

Cash a/c   Dr 7100

     To Debtor (Shyam) a/c 7100

Case 3

Discounted Bills Receivable

In case the Business discounts Bills of Exchange with a bank before Maturity, then it receives the amount due under bill (less discount) from bank and ceases to be the payee. When the bill matures, the bank presents the bill to the customer and receives payment.

Cash a/c Dr. 6750

Discount Fee a/c   Dr   250

       To Bills Receivable a/c   7000

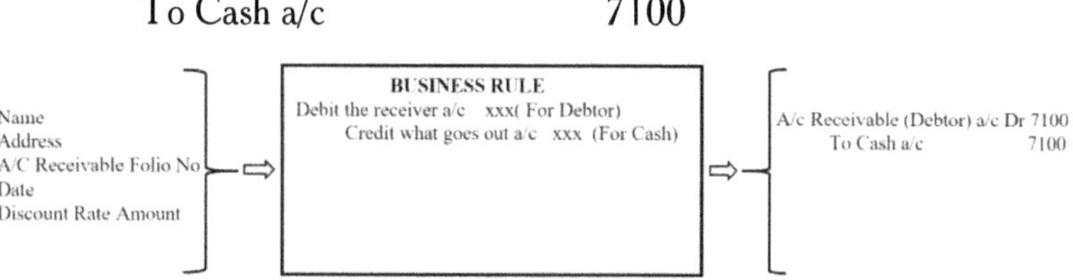

Case 4

Discounted Bill Dishonoured.

If the Customer fails to make the payment to the bank on maturity, then the bank can call the business to make the payment.

Accounts Receivable(Debtor)   a/c Dr.   7100 (7000+100)

      To Cash a/c   7100

Bills Receivable (Amount due from Customer) includes Noting Charges of Rs 100 from the bank.

The cash is paid to the bank to reimburse it for the dishonoured bill and to pay the noting charges.

11.7.2 <u>Terms of Payment</u>

When a document is processed, one needs to enter the terms of payment for the SAP ERP application to calculate the required conditions of payment.

The terms of payment are stored in the master record of a customer or a vendor. Terms of payment are conditions agreed upon by business partners for the payment of invoices.

Terms of payment define the following parameters:

- Due date

- Cash discount offered for payment of the invoice within a certain period

Some terms of payment are predefined in the ERP application. One can also add new terms of payment if required.

<u>Case 5</u>

XYZ Ltd sold goods worth Rs 5000 and offered a cash discount @ 10% if payment is made within 10 days of date of invoice and 2% discount for all the payments made after 10 days.

Cash a/c Dr.   4950

Discount allowed a/c Dr. 50

To Customer a/c   5000

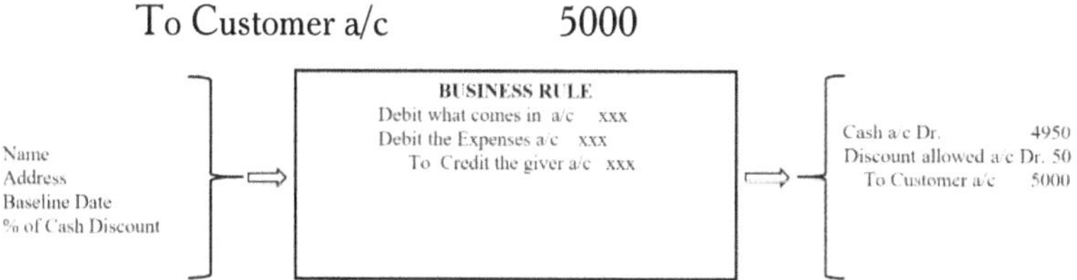

11.7.3 <u>Depreciation</u>

Charts of depreciation are used to manage various legal requirements for the depreciation and valuation of assets. Since charts of depreciation must be country-specific, ERP provides sample charts of depreciation for many countries. One can use these country-specific sample charts of depreciation to create your own company-specific chart of depreciation.

Each depreciation area represents a specific type of valuation, such as book depreciation or tax depreciation. One can also define one's own depreciation areas for a chart of depreciation.

Case 6

ABC Ltd bought machinery for Rs 3,00,000/- and installed in their factory in India on 30th September 2019.

As per Income Tax Act 1961, the rate of depreciation on machinery is 15% . The shelf life of the machinery is 10 yrs. The Asset Salvage value is Rs 50,000/-

1) As per Book Value Method

Original cost of Machinery = Rs 3,00,000

(-) Salvage Value   = Rs 50,000

Net Value of Asset   Rs 2,50,000

Amount of Depreciation per annum= $\dfrac{Rs\ 2,50,000}{10}$ = Rs 25,000/-

Since Machinery is purchased and installed on 30/09/2019, we shall charge the depreciation only for 6 months ,
that is, Rs 25000/2 = Rs 12,500/-

For F.Y 2019-20, A.Y 2020-21

31/03/2019 Depreciation a/c Dr 12,500

        To Machinery   12,500

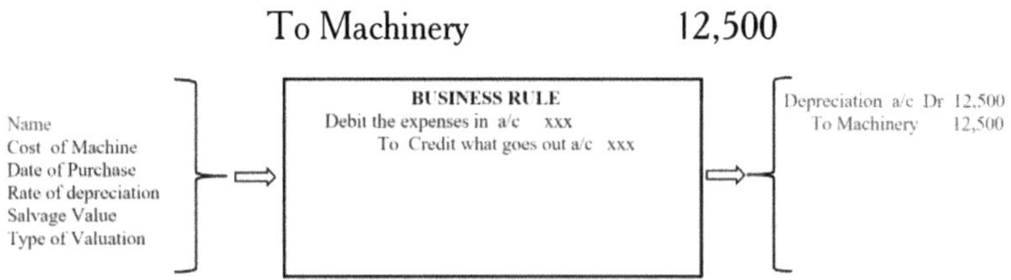

2) Depreciation under Income Tax Act ,1961

Original cost of Machinery = Rs 3,00,000

Amount of Depreciation per annum= Rs 3,00,000 @ 15% = Rs 45000/-

Since Machinery is purchased and installed on 30/09/2019, we shall charge the depreciation only for 6 months ,
that is,   Rs 45000/2 = Rs 22.,500/-

For F.Y 2019-20, A.Y 2020-21

31/03/2019 Depreciation a/c Dr 22,500

                        To Machinery   22,500

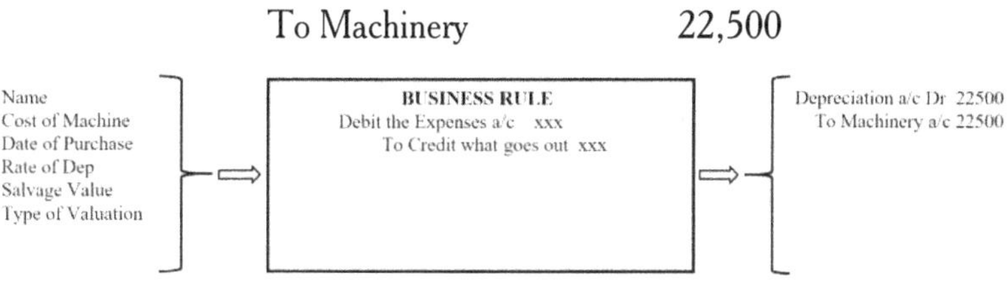

11.7.4 **Period Concept**

i) **Revenue Expenditure**

Prepaid expenses are expenses that you have paid in advance and posted in the fiscal year to be closed, but for accounting purposes, you need to assign in part or entirely to the new fiscal year because they represent future benefits.

Case 7

Mr. Roy hired a studio in Mumbai for a monthly rent of Rs 5000 on 01st February 2019. He made prepaid expenditure for 3 months as on 1[st]February 2019.

01/02/2019 Prepaid Rent a/c Dr   15000
                To Cash/ Bank a/c   15000
28/02/2019 Rent a/c Dr   5000
                Prepaid Rent a/c   5000
31/03/2019 Rent a/c Dr   5000
                To Prepaid Rent   5000
30/04/2019 Rent a/c Dr   5000
                To Prepaid Rent   5000

In the systems approach, the above case study is depicted as a typical process of accounting business process synthesis and integration as shown in the block diagram below

BUSINESS PROCESS SYNTHESIS AND INTEGRATION

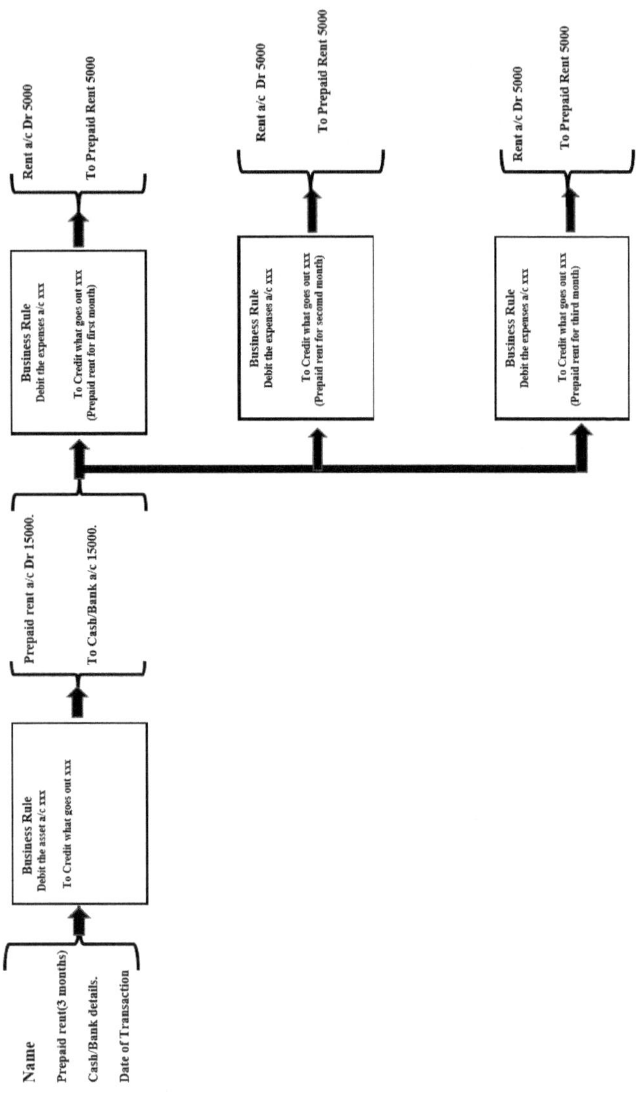

ii) <u>Accrued Expenses but not paid</u>

Mr. Shyam disbursed. salary of Rs 5000 to his employee on the first of every month.At the end of financial year the March salary is outstanding as the salary is disbursed on the 1st of April

31/03/2019 Salary a/c Dr 5000

> To Outstanding Salary 5000

01/04/2019 Outstanding salary a/c Dr 5000

> To Cash / Bank   5000

iii) <u>Capital Expenditure</u>

<u>Case 8</u>

Mr. Akash purchased a land for his factory for Rs 80 lakhs on 01/10/2021. He incurred costs for brokerage commission, survey fees, legal fees, property taxes, and expenditures for grading and clearing the land which total amounted to Rs 10 lakhs.

Here the entire costs incurred will be capitalised and added to the cost of the land.

Rs(in lakhs)

Land a/c Dr   90
  To Cash/Bank   90

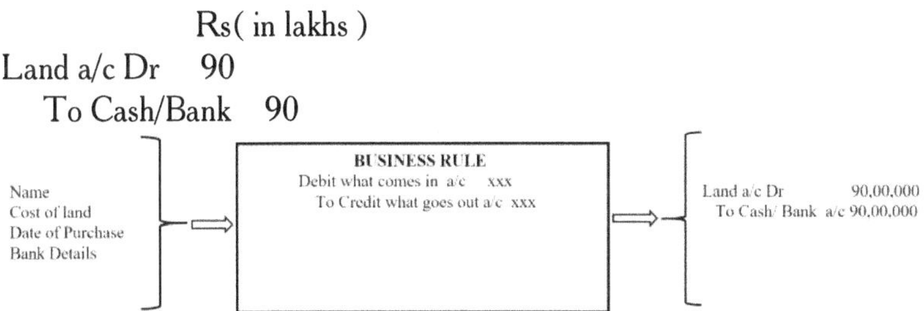

12.

Conclusion

To sum up, based on the experience of implementing a seamlessly integrated enterprise wide IT solution, the following points are recommended for consideration when an organisation is contemplating a major transformation in the operation of its business:

1. Business Process Re-engineering should be resorted to only if it is considered to be an absolute must.

2. It would be advisable to thoroughly understand the three Ts namely, the Technique (domain knowledge), Technology and Tools (platform, database, front end etc.) before attempting a corporate transformation.

3. If an external agency's assistance is felt necessary for the corporate transformation project, then it must be ensured that the agency has adequate domain knowledge.

4. A standard ERP package must be used only if it can be customised to provide a perfect fit for the business process.

5. For a large organisation with proven legacy systems, experience has shown that a standard ERP package does not provide a perfect fit. In such a case, it is still possible to put in position an enterprise-wide, seamlessly integrated, solution by using MIMOCODS system.

6. The following are the take-aways based on the case studies on the application of Artificial Intelligence/Machine Learning to commercial problems in shipping business:

i)A large number of training data sets of the order of 800 to 1000, is required to train the algorithm in a meaningful manner.

ii)A thorough knowledge of the business process and all its nuances is required for selecting the features for the hypothesis for accurate prediction or decision making.

iii) The process of selecting the features and training the algorithm followed by extensive testing and validation, is a time consuming process and is based on trial and error till an acceptable prediction model or hypothesis is achieved.

iv) Normally a large team consisting of business process experts with profound domain knowledge and a group of data science specialists work together as a team for the successful completion of AI/ML application projects.

Before signing off, here are some food for thought and a few tips for action:

FOOD FOR THOUGHT

A study about the operations of the famed dabbawalas (lunch box carriers) of Mumbai reveals that the dabbawalas make only one error in 16 million transactions which is way above the Six Sigma performance requirement of 3.4 defects per million opportunities. This hallmark figure of a single error in 16 million transactions which no entrepreneur in the world has ever achieved, has been achieved by the simple dabbawalas of Mumbai by their hard work, dedication to duty, common sense and profound domain knowledge. They do not use any sophisticated management techniques or software or gizmos for accomplishing the task. This stunning performance by the dabbawalas has left all the corporate giants gaping in disbelief. What's more, this incredible performance has earned them worldwide fame. So much so, that the BBC World aired on their TV channel a full length documentary on the dabbawalas' activity and achievement and not to be left behind in the race to accord recognition to them for their record breaking feat, one of the leading management institutes in Mumbai, invited the dabbawalas to share their experiences with the faculty members and students of business management. Doesn't this convey a lesson or two to the management gurus, corporate leaders and CEOs of FORTUNE 500 companies? The dabbawalas' mantra for success is **KISS (Keep It Simple and Straight!)**

THE PRINCE AND THE SHOWBOY

HE CAME ! HE SAW !! AND HE CONCURRED !!!

<u>TIPS FOR ACTION</u>

We conclude this essay with repeat of the quote from one of the vedas and possible lessons we can draw from it:

"Aa no bhadraah kratavo yantu vishvatah"

(-Rigveda 1-89-1)

is verse from the Rigveda which means:

"Let noble thoughts come to us from every side".

Paying heed to these pearls of wisdom, let us with an open mind accept noble thoughts , ideas, and suggestions on business management from every quarter irrespective of whether they originate from management gurus or from a simple dabbawala or for that matter from our mothers. Let us not forget that while technologies and tools are important for conducting business in today's highly competitive world , it is domain knowledge which will help us to stay ahead in the race.

BIBLIOGRAPHY

1. Ainapure Varsha and Ainapure Mukund- " Cost Accounting ",(Manan Prakashan, 2021)

2. Ainapure Varsha and Ainapure Mukund- "Accountancy and Financial Management",(Manan Prakashan, 2021)

3. Allen, RGD - "Mathematical Analysis for Economists", (Macmillan India Ltd., 1987).

4. Barry Povey – " Continuous Business Improvement", (McGraw Hill Company, England, 1996).

5. Chary, L.R -" BPR & THE 3Ts - Is there a future for Legacy Systems?", (BMA REVIEW - A Journal of the Bombay Management Association, Vol:15, No: 2, March - April 2004).

6. Chary, L R – "Corporate Transformation Without Tears", (The Institute of Marine Engineers(India), 2005).

7. Di Stefano, Joseph J, Stubberud, Allen R, Williams, Ivan J - "Feedback & Control Systems", (McGraw Hill Book Company, 1987).

8. Kuo, B C - "Automatic Control Systems", (Prentice - Hall of India Ltd., New Delhi, 1967).

9. Michael Hammar and James Champy – Reengineering The Corporation – A Manifest For Business Revolution, (Nicholas Brealey Publishing Ltd, London, 1993).

10. Nachane, DM and Chary, L R - "Posicast Control and Optimal Monetary Policy" - (Presented at the International Federation of Automatic Control/International Federation of Operations Research Society's Conference in June 1973 at Warwickshire, UK - Published in IEE Conference Proceedings No. 101).

11. Pontrjagin, LS et al - "The Mathematical Theory of Optimal Processes", (Interscience Publications, New York, 1962).

12. Stuart J. Russell and Peter Norvig – "Artificial Intelligence – A Modern Approach",(Pearson India Education Services Pvt Ltd, NOIDA, 2016).

13. Sandeep Desai and Abhishek Srivastava – " ERP to E^{2}RP- A CASE STUDY APPROACH"(Prentice Hall of India, 2013).

14. Tanenbaum, Andrews - "Computer Networks", (Pearson Education (Singapore) Pte. Ltd., Indian Branch, New Delhi, 2003)

15. Yadav, DS - "Foundations of Information Technology", (New Age International (P) Ltd., New Delhi, 2002).